PATINA
MODERN

PATINA MODERN

A Guide to Designing Warm, Timeless Interiors

Chris Mitchell and Pilar Guzmán

Artisan | New York
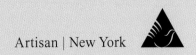

Contents

Foreword

I'VE SPENT THE BETTER PART OF MY CAREER PHOTOGRAPHING some of the most beautiful interiors around the world. While many of these homes—with their world-class art and furniture collections and painstakingly curated curios—are unassailable from a design perspective, it is a true rarity to find a house of this caliber that is also a home in the more traditional sense of the word: a space reflective of the taste and sensibilities of the owners, full of objects with meaning and history.

When I first walked into Chris and Pilar's home in Bridgehampton, I was immediately struck by its warmth and honesty. The materials were simple—a mixture of white oak, brass, and heavily patinated leather—and the overall design was full of nuance and elegance. Whether barstools by the slightly obscure 1960s California designer Cleo Baldon that Chris found at a flea market or the beautifully worn, centuries-old Kazak rug from Pilar's childhood home, the objects that surrounded me were personal and particular to them. Chris and Pilar were full of stories about every object on every shelf and the history of each piece of furniture, all of which had been collected over a lifetime of passionate connoisseurship.

And I quickly came to realize that their approach to decorating was driven not only by their connection to the decor but also by how they actually live within their home. No sooner had we started shooting than heaps of gorgeous charcuterie and bread appeared—not as props for the shoot, but for us to snack on outside of the camera frame. As we eased into the lunch hour, it became apparent that the "good china is for company" instinct most of us picked up from our parents didn't apply here. Chris and Pilar didn't hesitate to serve water out of a highly collectible Carl Auböck leather and brass decanter, salad greens from an eighteenth-century porcelain English bowl, and grilled fish from a mid-century Danish teak platter. When they learned that my wife and son happened to be in the neighborhood, they set two more places at the table and insisted that they join us for a delicious and casual family-style lunch. Soon after, my seven-year-old, feeling quite at home, fell asleep—wet swimsuit and all—on one of the daybeds, blissfully ignorant of its impressive pedigree. And it turns out, Chris and Pilar wouldn't have it any other way. The art of good design may hinge on excellent taste and careful curation, but their homes are a testament to the fact that it has just as much to do with how you live with and love the things that surround you.

—ADRIAN GAUT

What is Patina Modern?

TWENTY-FIVE YEARS AGO, PILAR AND I BROUGHT VERY different design sensibilities to our relationship. She grew up in Los Angeles, but contrary to stereotype, in a beloved Old English Tudor house filled with an eclectic mix of antiques. I was the professed modernist—a midwestern kid who had dreamed of living in a SoHo loft. From our first apartment together, and along the way through two New York City renovations and four in the Hamptons, our tastes merged surprisingly easily. In fact, this "your-peanut-butter-is-in-my-chocolate" collision turned out to be the basis of a design philosophy from which we haven't looked back.

By way of explanation, our favorite two buildings are the Glass House and the Rhinelander mansion. The former is as described: a low, sleek, steel and glass box that the architect Philip Johnson built for himself in Connecticut, in 1949. It's spare, rigorous, perfect modernism. The other is Ralph Lauren's original flagship store, on Madison Avenue in New York City—an impossibly grand, 1895 French-inspired château with plush carpets, polished mahogany, and equestrian paintings. In a word, both are equally transporting. But we're not sure we'd actually like to live in either. You see, we want rooms that are both spare *and* warm. Layered *and* clean. Current *and* timeless.

We think the formula for achieving this lies in mixing modern design with well-worn materials—thus creating interiors that feel a bit like the love child of those two iconic buildings. We've always been drawn to mid-century furniture, and our favorite pieces are those that are rendered in a limited palette of materials like white oak, aged brass, and bridle leather. What these elements have in common is that as they age, they become richer, mellower, burnished. Some things are best on their first day in the world. Not these.

Perhaps our favorite example of this combination at work is the leather banquette in our Brooklyn kitchen (see it on page 54). We designed it based on a 1940s Danish chair, which makes it very tailored and leggy and a bit formal. Over its fifteen-year lifetime, it has endured everything from papier-mâché accidents to wayward soy sauce, and this wear and tear has only made the piece better—aged in a way that no "distressing" treatment could ever replicate.

That's Patina Modern.

—CHRIS

This isn't your typical design book.

INTERIOR DESIGN IS HARD. OR AT LEAST IT SEEMS INTENDED to be. Most of us get tripped up by the wrong labels and the wrong questions. So much of the design jargon that gets thrown around in books and magazines and all over Instagram forces us to self-identify using terms like "traditional," "modern," "eclectic," or, our least favorite, "transitional."

And while we are all for a house with a clear design point of view that might hew to one tradition or another, and have utmost respect for rigorous modernists with nary a knickknack as well as die-hard maximalists who deftly mix ikat with toile, we find that both camps often forget the humans—with all their moods, hopes, and dreams—who do the actual living in these spaces.

We aren't professionals; we are self-taught, highly discerning design enthusiasts and collectors who have amassed, over the course of twenty years and six renovation and design projects, some hard-won wisdom. Our projects have been influenced by two things: a passion for twentieth-century design, and the groundbreaking work of our favorite designers. The goal of this book is to inspire you to identify the things you love, and to give you a few tools and guiding principles to help you put those pieces together into beautiful spaces.

We recognize how much pressure most of us put on ourselves to get it just right—to have our homes both protect and reflect us, to be the ever-evolving backdrop of the movie of our lives. See, we believe that the job of a home is twofold: to signal the aspirations of how we want to live on our best day, as well as to provide shelter to us, both practically and emotionally, along the messy road of life. We also believe that all houses have a soul. Some present it readily, while others require coaxing. The way we see it is that when we move into a home, we are entering into a relationship, a dance in which we balance our own needs with what the house wants to be. Not unlike marriage, designing a home requires the ongoing reconciliation of mutual hopes and dreams with baggage and limitations. But as you will see in the following pages, these limitations often proved to be our greatest gifts. If you like what we've done with our spaces, we think we can give you a playbook and the confidence to create a home that feels both modern and warm, both personal and photoworthy.

—PILAR

Our Manifesto

WE KNOW WHAT IT'S LIKE TO STARE AN EMPTY HOUSE IN THE eye in terror and try to figure out how to bring it to life. Creating a space that's beautiful, showcases personal taste and sensibilities, and works for real lives is daunting. Here are the design moves we live by.

1 MAINTAIN A LAYERED BUT LIMITED PALETTE.

Far from boring, a restrained mix of neutral tones and natural textures will add a calming, warm dimension to a room, without making it scream.

2 DON'T BE SCARED OF USING BLACK.

Black is the unsung accent that mixes with everything. It gives a room definition, like the effect of mascara on lashes. And precisely because it isn't a "color," black is a safe choice to offset softer neutrals.

3 GET YOUR SPACES TO GLOW.

We swear by lots of low-wattage lamps and sconces. In the evening, we want our rooms to feel like lanterns, both within and when viewed from afar.

4 THINK MOODS, NOT SCHOOLS.

We freely mix eras and styles in our rooms— we believe that interiors should be about creating a feeling, not rigidly adhering to set labels or lingo like "eclectic" or "mid-century."

5 TAKE A BIRD'S-EYE VIEW.

Our approach to furniture arrangements (and tableaus and tablescapes) is to think about how objects relate to one another from above. It's a good trick for avoiding a messy look, and it allows you to appreciate the interplay of objects.

6 COUNTERPROGRAM WHAT'S THERE.

What makes a room interesting is the tension between old and new, curvy and angular, rough and smooth, refined and elemental.

7 DESIGN FOR HOW YOU WANT TO LIVE.

Elegance and soulfulness are not mutually exclusive. Every room should be one you want to spend real time in. If it's designed to be off-limits to kids or pets, or to everyday living, what's the point?

8 CREATE ROOMS WITH MULTIPLE PURPOSES.

We love kitchens and bathrooms that feel as loungy as living rooms, dining rooms that double as libraries, dens that are office by day and screening room by night.

9 AND OF COURSE . . . EMBRACE PATINA.

Everything you bring into your home should get better with age. That doesn't mean you won't re-cover the sofa over time or sacrifice a piece that's finally worn to death, but if you buy something that you know looks best on its first day, it's just planned obsolescence.

Starting with Great Ingredients

THROUGHOUT OUR HOMES, WE HEW TO A LIMITED REPERTOIRE of materials and palette. Oak, leather, and brass are the real stars, supported by a cast of neutral colors and fabrics. As our collecting and decorating have evolved, we have found that these core materials are the constants in our favorite movements, styles, and periods. When we look for Danish or French antiques, the holy grail is a piece in oak that is held together with brass hardware and sports leather accents—the hat trick.

Why? The simple answer is because all three materials get better with age. To watch the pinkish hue of untanned bridle leather mellow and mottle is to see this material at its best. Likewise, the way an oak table dulls and softens at the edges from generations of family dinners, or a brass doorknob becomes burnished from the touch of a million turns—these are true things of beauty.

At the root of our appreciation of these objects' patina is our love of their authentic utility. It's no wonder that these materials—found in ships, saddles, and tools—are among the hardest working in history. Once in a while, we're lucky enough to find and salvage things like an actual naval bulkhead light or English equestrian slobber strap and use them in our renovations.

While these materials are the core of our design aesthetic, there is more in the mix—we pair them with a limited palette of fabrics, wall coverings, and other accessories that let these heroes stand out.

Oak

"IN A WORD, THE BEAUTY OF
THIS WOOD IS ITS HONESTY."

WE'RE MOSTLY TALKING ABOUT WHITE OAK, INCLUDING
Quercus alba in North America, *Q. robur* in Europe, and *Q. acutissima* in
Asia. Its pale warmth makes this hardwood work well almost everywhere,
from Versailles to MoMA. It's equally at home as a classic Paris apartment's
parquet floor, a modernist house's paneled walls, and a SoHo loft's beams.
In a word, the beauty of this wood is its honesty.

A naturally dense and resilient wood that doesn't splinter like its red
oak cousin, white oak was historically the chief material for everything
from clipper ships to Japanese *bokken*. Due to its natural abundance in
England and France, white oak was once the region's dominant building
material, and today, the oldest of these durable timbers are often found
in framing and in flooring, their wide planks softened and grooved by
centuries of footfalls. The simplicity of this material also shines through in
French country furniture, such as worktables worn by palms and marked
by tools. In more refined, deco pieces from 1930s France, we see cerusing,
the applying and subsequent wiping off of white paint, which highlights
oak's grain. Perhaps the material's greatest fans were French designers
Robert Guillerme and Jacques Chambron, whose entire oeuvre, from beds
to credenzas to lighting, was rendered in oak.

Over in Denmark, soap-finished oak gives a cool, matte touch to iconic
pieces like Hans Wegner's Wishbone chair and Børge Mogensen's Spanish
chair. The Danish cabinetmakers of the mid-century period were truly the
masters of woodcraft, with highly figured details, elaborate joinery, and thin
profiles. Yet there's an essential honesty in even the finest examples when
they are rendered in oak. Today, Danish oak pieces are more desirable for
their scarcity—an irony because it was the modesty of the material that
made oak less prized at the time. (The relative rarity of teak and, greater
still, Brazilian rosewood meant that those were the preferred materials for
most Danish mid-century pieces, resulting in greater inventory today.) From
refined to rustic and sculptural to slab, solid, unflappable oak is literally and
figuratively foundational to our interiors.

Brass

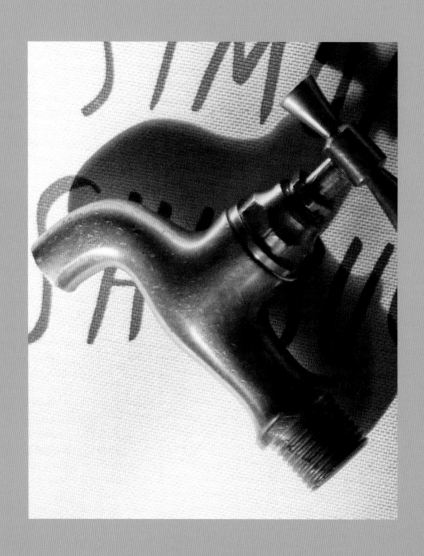

"THE OILS AND WEAR OF TOUCH MOTTLE THE SURFACE WITH A RANGE AND DEPTH OF COLOR THAT SHOW THIS MATERIAL AT ITS BEST."

BRASS, LIKE BRONZE, WAS MADE TO AGE. AS ITS SURFACE oxidizes, it loses its shine and darkens to a warm brown, and the oils and wear of touch mottle the surface with a range and depth of color that show this material at its best.

As the exclusive material for maritime use, naval brass—with its metallurgist combination of copper, zinc, and tin—holds up to the corrosive salt air of the sea. Not surprisingly, many of our favorite brass pieces are the chunky antique cleats and bollards from ships and sailboats.

As a design element, brass is used as both fittings and objets. The hundreds of trays, paperweights, and follies by Carl Auböck are almost exclusively in brass or bronze. Other designers reserved brass for smaller runs of popular steel objects, like Arne Jacobsen's ash bowls. In Sweden, for Skultuna, Pierre Forssell honored the schnapps tradition best with his rocking decanter, along with the architectural precision of his counterweighted candlesticks. In Germany, the sculptural forms of Florian Schulz's Posa pendants and helmet table lamps give a jewelry-like quality to these items.

Danish designers carried the naval tradition of hardware into their furniture, using brass as hinges, table supports, drawer locks, and more. The cleat-like locks on a Børge Mogensen model 232 cabinet from the 1960s are both modern and the ultimate homage to the material's past. In Italy, designers like Ignazio Gardella and Osvaldo Borsani added key brass accents to their sexy postwar pieces with levers and adjusters. The reclining handle on Borsani's airline-like P40 lounge chair gives the piece a solidity and heft. In Gardella's highly sought-after Digamma series, the duck-like feet and side adjusters provide a warmth that steel would sorely lack. Even more dramatic are his mahogany bookcases, whose supports wear long brass "shoes" and whose shelves are pinned with heavy round bolts. Overtly or not, any brass accent or fitting nods to its nautical or industrial roots, conferring a level of honesty, utility, and historicity even to the most whimsical of objects.

Leather

"IT IS THE STAINS, BLOTCHES, AND MOTTLES OF TIME THAT GIVE VEGETABLE-DYED LEATHER A DEEPLY IMPERFECT BUT SATISFYING PATINA."

HERE'S THE THING ABOUT VEGETABLE-TANNED LEATHER:
it stains. That's hard for many people, because unlike oak or brass, the
patina can't be sanded off or polished away. Vegetable-tanned leather, so
named because the tannins used to dye it come from organic matter like
tree bark and plants, ranges in color from bone to beige to an almost petal
pink in its original state. With the oils and oxidation of everyday touch and
air, the hide takes on a range of tones, mellowing from light tan to deep
chestnut. But this process defies uniformity—and it is the stains, blotches,
and mottles of time that give vegetable-dyed leather a deeply imperfect but
satisfying patina.

Like oak and brass, vegetable-tanned leather is also wholly practical.
Since this tanning process produces the sturdiest leather, it has long been
used for saddles and other bridle tack, holsters and other military supplies,
and suitcases and travel trunks. The wear of an Hermès saddle or a Louis
Vuitton trunk, from those luxury companies' earliest days as tack or travel
providers, proved so beautiful that they form the basis of their current
offerings. An Hermès Birkin bag is the direct descendant of a saddle, just
as a Vuitton Nomade duffel is the progeny of a steamer trunk.

In design, it is the Danes who dominate this material. The hard
sling of a Børge Mogensen chair, the expanse of Poul Kjærholm's PK80
daybed mattress, and the Kaare Klint Safari pieces all show off vegetable-
tanned leather to its fullest. With his Egg and Swan chairs, Arne Jacobsen
demonstrated how this tough material can also be sensuous.

When used as an accent, this leather adds a warmth that's unrivaled.
The Parisian designer Jacques Adnet made a career of wrapping chair
legs, lamps, and metal furniture in vegetable-tanned leather. As piping and
covered-button accents, it lends tailoring to Flemming Lassen and Arnold
Madsen sheepskin chairs. And as pulls on a Kurt Østervig credenza, it's a
pliable decoration on a simple form. In our own projects, we love how this
material hearkens equally to the traditions of equestrian riding and fine
luggage. Is there anything more luxurious?

Palette

AS ESSENTIAL AS OAK, BRASS, AND LEATHER ARE TO OUR aesthetic, so too is the environment in which they shine. One of our guiding principles is that these materials, precisely because they patinate, are deep and nuanced colors in their own right, better than anything mixed in a paint can or dyed on a fabric. That's why we love to let them stand out in rooms that are otherwise neutral.

But designing a neutral palette is not as simple as putting a coat of white paint on everything and calling it a day. We tend to favor a more layered palette of cool whites, flaxy taupes, green-grays, and charcoals. Each, in its own way, highlights the pale beauty of oak, embraces brass's warm shine, and complements rich leather tones.

PAINT & WALL COVERINGS

Big color statements not only tend to date quickly, but we've also found that the joy wears off for the homeowner who sees them every day. Many a friend's red dining room became a cautionary tale. Instead, we lean toward more muted tones (Farrow & Ball's Ammonite, Worsted, and Pavilion Gray are warm and light without being too stark), then reserve our more adventurous choices for bold accents like a throw pillow, an occasional chair, or art.

We also love letting exterior greenery be the color in our rooms: as Martha Stewart taught Pilar, using neutrals and grays instead of pure white allows the eye to focus on the view outside.

When we have taken the plunge with a bolder color, we've gravitated toward shades that are deep rather than vibrant, and paired them with darker neutrals so as to avoid the shock of contrast. The dark green-gray of our Brooklyn kitchen works precisely because it marries well with the warmth of the mahogany woodwork and leather upholstery.

TEXTILES & RUGS

A cast of neutral fabrics adds the layering that makes deceptively clean rooms feel so rich. We look for materials and colors found in nature: curly sheepskin, flax linen, cashmere flannel, woven jute. These and others are favorites for how nuanced they are within such a limited palette, and for their ability to add texture to modern interiors. We also look to tailoring for inspiration: dressing a room is akin to dressing a person, and like a gray flannel suit, a sofa in the same fabric offers a sophisticated but cozy feel.

Often, it's the variety of these materials that allows them to complement one another so well. The roughness of a jute log basket or area rug provides the right contrast to the buttery softness of a cashmere throw. The stuffed-animal puffiness of shearling cushions counterprograms the sharp lines of whatever wood or steel furniture frames they sit on.

ACCENTS

Consistently, we find that black is the best accent, for its dramatic contrast and monochromatic restraint. One tends to forget that black is a neutral that when used sparingly or in a supporting role (in pillows, objects, trimmings, and even molding) creates the right design tension. It can add a sharpness to soft rooms, and a dose of modern to offset traditional light neutrals.

JAMES WHITE°   2010

SAVAGE GROUND°   213

STONY GROUND° 211   CORD°

8

OLD WHITE°   4

DROP CLOTH°   283

LIGHT GRAY°   17

House on a Hill

"It was our shared dream, largely unspoken, and hardly an original one, to have our adult life play out in a house where coming home meant opening one's own front door to a safe, stolid haven—a respite in the middle of the city, shoulder to shoulder with its stately, handsome neighbors."

WE MET IN NEW YORK, BOTH HAVING MOVED
here after college in Berkeley, California. During those early
years, we spent most of our time at Pilar's apartment in the
West Village. In the evenings, we
would walk around that jewel-box
neighborhood, coveting the brick
row houses with their warm light,
tall rooms, and domestic scenes
unfolding inside. It was our
shared dream, largely unspoken,
and hardly an original one, to
have our adult life play out in a
house like that. Where coming
home meant opening one's
own front door to a safe, stolid
haven—a respite in the middle of
the city, shoulder to shoulder with
its stately, handsome neighbors.

    A few years later, when
we were ready to enter the cage
match that is New York City real
estate, the luxuries on our list
were modest: just not tiny by
Manhattan standards, and a few
direct rays of sunlight at some
point in the day. We didn't dare
wish for things like a fireplace or
a terrace, much less our own front door. We had just started
our search when we found a *New York Times* listing—our
first introduction to the words "estate condition." To the
uninitiated—namely, us—that sounds promising (on the
basis that anything qualifying as an estate must be good).
In fact, it means that in all likelihood the previous owner

died there, and that large discolored area on the dining room floor should be treated suspiciously. We saw the apartment, a "classic five" in New York parlance, during its first (and only) open house. What greeted us and the other prospective buyers was a scene of such grime, filth, and general junkyard conditions that any description wouldn't do it justice. But where the others apparently saw tetanus, we saw deep moldings, generously sized rooms, a long and elegant hallway. We saw paneled doors, multiple fireplaces, pocket shutters. We saw home.

And so began our love affair with renovating old homes, a series of leaps both financially headlong and seriously dubious to our friends and family.

A few years after this first renovation adventure succeeded way beyond our modest hopes, we hatched a plan with Chris's younger brother, Gregg, and his wife, Andrea, to buy a town house and create two homes. It was like a cheat code in the game of New York real estate: here was our chance to lay our hands on a house through a shared mortgage. There was one place on Stuyvesant Street—an *Age of Innocence* block of the East Village that dripped with period charm. That house proved impossible not only for its narrow, 15-foot (4.6 m) width but also for its many rent-controlled inhabitants who would clearly outlast us, in fortitude if not in years. But then Gregg and Andrea proffered the next move: a listing for yet another estate-condition house, this one in Park Slope, Brooklyn. In this case, that two-word descriptor meant stacks of old newspapers that completely filled some of the rooms, peeling bordello-red walls, rotting window casings, and the questionable structural integrity of its entire right half.

But we refused to be daunted by any of that. Having seen these kinds of row houses only by peering in from the outside—and conditioned as we were to New York apartments—we found ourselves overwhelmed by the scale and detail of this 1880s brownstone. Through the double doors of the vestibule, past the thick mahogany front door, we were greeted by a 10-foot (3 m) hall tree and easily the fattest balustrade we'd ever seen. It was there that we had a clear vision of adoring future children racing down those stairs to greet their weary parents as we returned home in the evening.

And so, in the middle of a snowstorm, we all met to confirm our collective love for this wreck. We walked around the corner to a burrito joint to hammer out the details, and embarked on our greatest adventure to date.

When we became the third owners of this house, we took over from an Italian American family who had lived there for more than fifty years. Successive generations had not been kind to the place, carving it up into multiple apartments, each with its own series of deadbolts on the original bedroom doors.

Baptized as we were from our previous renovation, we set about restoring this house to its former elegance. We agreed that Gregg and Andrea would take the garden floor, the simplest way to divide the brownstone and preserve separate entrances. Once that was settled, we tackled the big and boring stuff on the upper floors, like adding a header beam to gird the structure, snaking ducts throughout for air-conditioning, and replacing all the plumbing and wiring. Finally, we could turn our attention to the visible parts: in addition to installing a new kitchen and bathrooms, we replastered the walls and ceilings and refinished much of the mahogany woodwork. We kept the layout pretty much intact, though we tweaked it a bit, like commandeering a small room next to our bedroom for a more generous suite, and carving out a compact laundry room from two closets.

Throughout the project, our youth, naivete, and limited budget meant that we had to be scrappy and invent things as we went along. We chose our bathtub when we happened on a discounted Agape model with a minor flaw. And we borrowed our friend Tyler's construction crew, who were as ingenious as they were unorthodox. In the early aughts, even in a landmarked neighborhood, you could file a construction permit for "scraping and painting," then embark on a full-scale renovation. Because a Dumpster out front might give us away, our motley construction crew stacked all the old lathe and plaster and other debris in our living room, then secreted it out in early-morning van loadings. To this day, we don't know (nor want to) where they dumped all that material. To suggest the Gowanus Canal might not be a stretch.

After a year, which still seems remarkably fast to us, we moved in.

Park Slope

Home Tour: Light Within Heavy

AS THE PAINTED LADY CLAPBOARD IS TO SAN FRANCISCO, so is the brownstone to Brooklyn. They line blocks upon blocks of our Park Slope neighborhood, making it a perennial set for TV and movie shoots re-creating the Gilded Age through the Depression era.

From our earliest days in the city, we loved the idea of living in one of these stately homes. What we didn't realize were the constraints of row-house living. The obvious up-and-down of the levels we found charming, but the long-and-narrow footprint proved a real design challenge. So did the Victorian moldings, a curse as much as a blessing. Here is how we created our Patina Modern aesthetic within the confines of narrow rooms and heavy wood detailing.

Opposite: The view into the kitchen from the dining room. The coordinating chandeliers are a pair of counterweighted mobiles from David Weeks, a friend since the 1990s whose pieces we have hung in every one of our houses. They have become classics to us, neither trendy nor dated. Their Calder-like quality and delicate sway are perhaps the greatest counterprogramming we did to offset the lugubrious moldings.

Above: The original built-in closet was
converted to a bay that houses the Miele oven
and our collection of copper cookware.

THE KITCHEN

The brownstone is laid out in the traditional manner, with a front and rear parlor on the main level. Our first big move was to locate the kitchen in the rear parlor: it's a square room with a high ceiling, so an ideal space in which to convene (as we all tend to do in kitchens). What had been a set of closets flanking a glass-front bookcase became, respectively, space for the oven and a Sub-Zero fridge. The closet doors were saved (and repurposed for our en suite bath—see page 84). And the bookcase was refitted with subway tile we salvaged from an upstairs bathroom. With new hardware and glass shelves, it became a display for our collection of Raymond Loewy china (see page 92).

We anchored the room with a workhorse of an island that's home to a minimalist Gaggenau cooktop, a sink, a dishwasher, and the sum total of our food storage. The idea was to make the room feel open and light-filled, so we kept cabinetry to a minimum and left fully half the room for lounging.

On the opposite wall, we restored the fireplace and flanked it with a pair of banquette-style sofas. These are trim but comfy, and they maximize the footprint of the room. One of the banquettes is a corner unit, with an Eero Saarinen dining table where we eat pretty much every family meal—and have hosted a good many compact dinner parties.

In a counterintuitive move, since we were all about lightening up this house, we painted the kitchen walls in Farrow & Ball's Down Pipe. This dark gray-green allowed the white ceiling, with its deep moldings, to really pop, and it mellowed all the mahogany woodwork, which tonally complements instead of heavily contrasting with it. The result is a room that feels less like a kitchen and more like a study. Its original use as a less formal "parlor" turned out to be exactly what we re-created a hundred years later.

Leaning into Existing Detail

Repurposing the existing bookcase and woodwork in what was to become our kitchen didn't seem like a no-brainer at the time—we were used to traditional counter-height and upper cabinets. But once we realized we would have enough storage in the island and could use the alcove as an appliance counter and additional shelving, we embraced the original room-width woodwork and beveled glass doors. What we ended up with exceeded our greatest hopes, as the detail of the cabinet is a great counterpoint to the more modern island and stainless steel appliances, and the lighted glass shelves prove a dramatic showcase for china, glassware, and other collected finds.

Above: A pair of Enzo Mari fruit prints is a playful and graphic foil to the kitchen's antique woodwork.

Following pages: We cajoled our friend Tyler Hays, the founder of cult furniture maker BDDW, to design our Claro walnut island.

Above: The corner banquette, where we've had
most meals for the past eighteen years, was
inspired by a Kaare Klint design (see page 88).

Opposite: We love "found art." This tattered
original Italian poster, from a 1971 concert
documentary, is as much about the graphic
statement as it is about the band.

IL FILM PIU' ATTESO

PINK

FLOYD

A POMPEI

UNA ESCLUSIVITA' CINEPOP

THE LIVING AND DINING ROOMS

One of the challenges of brownstones is their relatively narrow width. With the space taken by the front hall and staircase, you end up with a bowling lane of a living room. Our solution was to create two areas—one for dining, closer to the kitchen, and a proper sitting area by the front windows.

Since the heavy mahogany moldings and pier mirror seem to close in the rooms even further, we knew that traditional antiques were off-limits. We saw so many brownstones around us that seemed a bit fusty and museum-like. And while we love the mix of old and new, here we felt that we had to leaven the weight of the Victorian with cleaner lines and thinner profiles, while balancing shapes and styles that might appear contradictory. Rather than crowding the side walls of the sitting area with upholstered furniture, we mounted a glass-front Danish cabinet on one wall and hung a massive, framed Japanese textile on the opposite side to give the room a graphic punch. Under that textile, we placed a small rosewood dresser and an Arne Jacobsen Swan chair. Rounding out the seating area is a two-piece travertine table from the 1980s that gives the space a harder edge, softened by a wool bouclé love seat.

Two elements that help lighten the parlor floor (both in hue and weight) are the David Weeks chandelier and the hand-knotted rug, which we designed and commissioned from a Tibetan weaver.

Opposite: The bouclé love seat is by CB2. Its curved back and diminutive size allow it to tuck neatly into the front bay of the living room.

Following pages: Our dining area is a small feat of spatial relations, with its 10-foot (3 m) BDDW oak Parsons table and Guillerme et Chambron chairs, and flanking Arne Vodder rosewood credenzas.

ROBERT STILIN

Opposite: A Tyler Hays painting hangs above the credenza, with a Thomas O'Brien Long Box sconce that has become one of our go-to fixtures (the substantial, square-shaded book cloth lamp, also by Thomas O'Brien, is now sadly discontinued).

Above: A collection of bisque pottery sits atop the second credenza below the salon wall. The pieces make more of a statement when clustered in numbers and are a nice hit of white against the wood.

Curating a Salon Wall

We developed this wall over time with one organizing principle: each artwork had to be created by or feature one of our family members. It includes everything from an oil portrait of Pilar's grandfather by her father to preschool drawings by our boys. We kept the frame profiles consistent but purposely mixed gilt, walnut, and ebonized woods. We love the way dimensional objects punctuate framed works, so we crowned the wall with an assortment of nineteenth-century Austrian mounts and Italian land-mine markers from World War II.

Counterprogramming with Color

Our living room and kitchen walls were initially painted white, in an effort to lighten up the dark effect of the Victorian woodwork. Eventually we realized that white wasn't the only way to cue "modern" and that the living room was better without so much contrast. A lineny Farrow & Ball shade called Elephant's Breath provided a much calmer, more composed space. In the kitchen, contrast was just what we were after: Farrow & Ball's Down Pipe, a dark gray-green hue, was used to offset the white ceiling and graphic artwork.

Above: A hanging oak credenza houses the overflow of our Raymond Loewy table service (see page 92). The pair of mirrors is by Uno & Östen Kristiansson.

Opposite: This Arne Jacobsen Swan chair was our first big furniture purchase, some twenty years ago, and we have never found its patinated leather more beautiful than we do today. The graphic simplicity of the monumental framed *boro* fragment is a perfect counterpoint to the ornate pier mirror. Both offer a reflective surface that bounces light into the middle of the parlor.

Following pages: A skylight bathes the stairwell in soft light.

THE DEN

Sometimes we think we're the last people (or at least the last generation) to keep books. Though we're avid collectors (see page 164), we wouldn't classify this as a "collection." It's too hardworking for that. Collections are about the hunt first, then the display and appreciation. Our library is composed of seemingly endless rows of cookbooks (every one of which Pilar has made a meal from), an ever-growing stack of art and design volumes we constantly return to for inspiration, and our favorite novels and biographies that are just now getting a third or fourth read by our sons. And so it was that we filled the entire rear wall of our den with a white oak bookcase.

We wanted this room to have a lounge-like glow at night. We achieved that by placing darker shaded lighting throughout: a pair of small lamps in the bookcase, a brass and Perspex lamp from Temde Leuchten on the desk, and a metal mushroom lamp by Hillebrand on the side table.

Since we use this room as our primary family movie-watching space as well as our study, we knew it needed both a large sofa and a large desk. The desk is by Osvaldo Borsani, and we had originally bought two of them to furnish our respective corporate offices. When the company moved its headquarters, we saved one desk for this space. Any time the weather dips below 50°F (10°C) is a good enough excuse to make a wood fire and work by its glow.

We leaned into darker tones of taupe, charcoal, and rosewood to give the den a moodier feel. A B&B Italia Charles sofa in wool flannel anchors the room. The rosewood Aksel Kjersgaard console and "marine edge" square coffee table have substance and warmth from the rich tones of the wood, but they're sleek and trim. We felt license to add these darker pieces here because it wouldn't be competing with dark brown woodwork, as elsewhere in the house; upon stripping the painted moldings and mantel in the den, we decided to stain it black instead of restoring the mahogany finish. The result is a clean, sharp contrast. Cool beige walls, a white ceiling, and black woodwork make for a classic palette: it's the khakis, white button-down, and black loafers of rooms.

Opposite: One of a pair of Osvaldo Borsani P40 lounge chairs upholstered in a Kvadrat wool. The rug is among three we designed in different colorways, all with calligraphic swirls inspired by artist Elliott Puckette's signature painting style.

Following pages: By anchoring the massive Borsani desk behind the sofa, we dramatically increased the usable space in the room and created both a great source of sofa reading light as well as an intimacy between someone on the couch and someone at the desk.

Above: A floating wall-to-wall custom
bookcase holds our entire working library.

Opposite: The rosewood coffee table has a
raised lip, or "marine edge"—so called for a
maritime detail that ensures things don't roll
off when on the high seas. It's a workhorse that
doubles as a dining table during movie nights.

Following pages, left: A collection of Swedish
and German brutalist pottery. We love the
rough textures and added elements like the
rope and chain.

Following pages, right: A 1970s Swiss lamp,
with a Perspex helmet shade that mimics
tortoise.

GRANDMA'S ROOM

Our requirements for any guest bedroom are
serenity and quiet, but especially so for the one
we reserve for Pilar's mother. We sought to offset
the abundance of polished woodwork with our
most limited palette yet. The goal was to envelop
the space in a sense of calm, with matching flannel
drapes, rug, and walls in a single shade of taupe
gray. The Claro walnut bed and side tables by
BDDW pick up the wood tones and give the room
an organic influence.

We kept the art to a minimum, with small
framed drawings beside the bed, and a long-held
Japanese exhibition poster that catalogs every
chair Hans Wegner designed. In a nod to this
being "Grandma's room," we hung a nineteenth-
century portrait that we found at the Paris flea
market. Floating art in a tonally painted frame is
a nice hack for modernizing and elevating older
or humbler works.

Above: This room is a study in neutrals. Wool
drapery and linen bedding complement the
taupe walls.

Opposite: The three-legged teak Danish stool
is an anonymous version of a Mogens Lassen
tractor stool, and the tabletop mirror is by Uno
& Östen Kristiansson.

Hans J Wegner

THE GUEST BATH

When we started our renovation, we tried desperately to save the original subway tile that half-lined the walls of this bathroom. But too many were damaged, and patching in new ones would have been obvious, so we decided to save them another way: we used them as the back walls of our kitchen's pantry nook and china cabinet (see page 53), then covered the whole bathroom with new tile. The result is floor-to-ceiling white porcelain, offset by the original deep bathtub painted Farrow & Ball's Off-Black, and new nickel hardware from Lefroy Brooks.

Over the years, we've experimented with various pieces of furniture in this room, from a simple stool to a carved Spanish trunk; at one point, we added a rosewood dressing table and mirror by Aksel Kjersgaard. Placing furniture, and especially antiques, in a bathroom is one way we like to offset the utilitarian nature of these purpose-driven rooms, making them feel a little more elevated and decorated.

Opposite: In the room's current iteration, a stool in black walnut by Sawkille adds a stark contrast to the white porcelain and tile.

Above: A deco porcelain washstand serves as a vanity in the guest bath. We love how it bridges antique and modern sensibilities.

THE PRIMARY BEDROOM

We knew we wanted our bedroom to have the feeling of a hotel suite, so we knocked down the wall to a small adjoining room in order to capture space for the bed and nightstands. This newfound sleeping nook creates a cozy area that opens to the larger area. This is possibly the only place in the house where we'd trust a cream-colored floor covering, and one by BDDW adds to the sweet serenity.

A porcelain washstand near the fireplace serves as a dressing table, and beyond the door is Chris's walk-in closet—a space that Pilar has dubbed "the haberdashery" for its fastidious organization and the manner in which it looks like a well-appointed, if pocket-size, men's shop.

Squeezing Storage into an Old House

We had initially intended to add a small settee or sofa to the foot of the bed, a look we've long admired. But we realized these old houses are short on storage, so we anchored the sleeping area instead with an antique English oak trunk from Pilar's childhood home. It's ideal for our bed linens and hard luggage, and it has long been a place the kids perch when they come talk to us in the morning.

The same lesson was applied to a recessed alcove in the den. It was, for years, a picture-perfect reading nook, with English floral upholstery and a wall of family photos. But as our kids grew, we were soon bursting at the seams for closet space (and realized that no one actually read there). So we converted the nook to a vestibule of sorts, with a coatrack and a wall of custom oak millwork closets that match the bookcase (see page 68).

Opposite: The brick wall behind the bed, painted the same Benjamin Moore Decorator's White as the rest of the room, was lightly plastered to retain its texture.

Following pages: A pair of antique brass nautical scissor lamps serves as bedside reading lights.

Above: An antique porcelain washstand serves
as a dressing table, replete with a folding teak
mirror by Kai Kristiansen. A delicate 1950s
Italian wall lamp, with its elegant ball-bearing
mechanism, hangs over the tableau like a
statement necklace.

Opposite: Perhaps nothing illustrates our
weakness for collecting and arranging more
than the items displayed on the washstand: all
manner of vintage sterling and crystal, knives,
flasks, leather cuff-link boxes, and other
trinkets that recall a bygone era.

THE PRIMARY BATH

One side effect of reserving the top floor of the house for our family bedrooms is that our sons have largely shared our bathroom their whole lives (we lacked the foresight when we had just one infant to plan for another bath up here). It's a testament to Pilar's saintliness that she continues to willingly share her bathroom with the boys.

We can't blame them for wanting to share it with us, though. Not only is it closer than the perfectly fine version one flight down, but it is also one of the most serene and prettiest spaces in the house.

The Agape Spoon tub sits under a large skylight, the shower tucks discreetly behind a corner, and the Claro walnut and brass medicine cabinet was another original custom-made gem by Tyler Hays. But the crowning achievement of this room is the 9-foot (2.7 m) pair of mahogany doors that was repurposed from the rear parlor closets in what is now the kitchen. They open up the whole room to our bedroom for a full "hotel suite" experience.

Repurposing (Almost) Everything

When we took the huge mahogany doors off the rear parlor closets, we knew we had to use them somewhere. They now form a dramatic double-wide entrance to the primary bath. With appropriate reciprocity, when the antique subway tile in the guest bath proved too damaged for us to keep it in place, we gingerly removed as much as we could and used it to line the walls of the kitchen alcove and china cabinet. The effect, with its charcoal grout and authentic spider cracks (no crackle glaze here!), lends an aged feel to the newly converted room. (Just about the only period detail we haven't figured out a use for is the giant wood dumbwaiter pulley that lived inside one of those closets. It still sits in the cellar, waiting for inspiration to hit.)

Opposite: Because the bathroom has no windows, we installed a large skylight to bring in some sun. In combination with the skylight, this tub might be the ultimate example of counterprogramming the traditional: it's the polar opposite of a Victorian claw-foot.

Design Notes

∧ FARROW & BALL ELEPHANT'S BREATH This paint is a really good beige that we've used over the years. It's warm and light without being too pink or too green and a better choice than a stark white against dark moldings. (For more on paint, see page 39.)

∧ TABLEAUS We are collectors of all kinds of things. Seashells, silver boxes and flasks, bridle leather anything. Grouping like objects is a good way to showcase your collections, but scale can also be an important organizing principle and make for fun vignettes, as with this idiosyncratic grouping on our washstand (see page 83).

> JAPANESE TEXTILE Big "found art" statements are good counterprogramming for the formality of a brownstone. This antique *boro* textile from Japan, emblazoned with a family crest, is a dramatic gesture for the parlor-height living/dining room.

∧ FAMILY CHRISTMAS CARD
A family portrait by Pilar's dad that he
sent, along with a note, to his relatives
in Chile was discovered decades later,
stuffed in the back of a drawer at his
home outside Santiago.

∧ PINK FLOYD POSTER Chris tracked
down a rare copy of a Pink Floyd in Pompeii
poster, which we hung in our kitchen. Its
bright palette pops against the room's dark
paint and wood.

> FINN JUHL 45 CHAIR
Perhaps the most revered of
the iconic Danish chairs, the
45 sits like a big lounger but
takes up minimal space.

∧ HEAVY BELGIAN LINEN For curtains
in the living room and our bedroom, we
opted for a heavy linen, with its pronounced
warp and weft, to add a rustic contrast to the
Victorian detail.

<∧ LEATHER BANQUETTE
We used the Kaare Klint Addition
sofa shown at left as inspiration for
our custom banquette, fabricated by
upholsterer Andrew Camp. We had
him alter the proportions to dining
height and made it a little deeper for
after-dinner lounging.

∨ HANS WEGNER DAYBED
FOR GETAMA We use this like an
upholstered bench, anchoring one
side of a seating area to delineate the
space without obstructing sight lines.

< ENZO MARI *APPLE* AND
PEAR PRINTS These graphic
posters knock down the formality
of the woodwork.

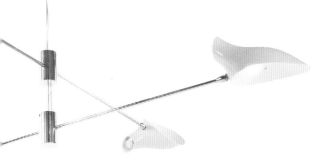

< ARNE JACOBSEN SWAN CHAIR This chair is, in many ways, the origin story of *Patina Modern*. We fell in love with it twenty-five years ago. It had a gorgeous patina to begin with, and after years of kids swiveling on it, the leather has sadly gotten more brittle, but also more beautiful. We wouldn't trade it for ten new ones.

∧ DAVID WEEKS CHANDELIER We love the mobile-like quality of this fixture. And its lightness is a good counterpoint to heavy moldings.

> KAY BOJESEN DANISH TEAK ANIMALS Someone gifted us a vintage monkey when our first son was born. While this beautifully crafted creature started out solo in the nursery, we gave him some siblings and moved him and a new species (the elephant) to the bookshelf in our den.

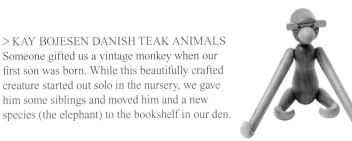

< GOOP X CB2 LOVE SEAT The mid-century-inspired love seat is the perfect cocktail-hour perch. The rounded back works with the angle of the bay window, nestling nicely in the corner without taking up the full width—ideal for these hard-to-furnish long and narrow Victorian brownstone front parlors.

< ∧ TRAVERTINE TABLE BY UP&UP Like other Italian designs from the 1970s and '80s, these triangular coffee tables fell out of favor but have since become quite collectible. They can be configured in myriad ways to fit a square or rectangular space.

∨ BORSANI P40 CHAIRS These endlessly configurable lounge chairs feel more like a first-class airplane seat than a traditional recliner.

<∧ BOOK CLOTH LAMPS These lamps from Thomas O'Brien (from Aero Studios, above, and a discontinued Visual Comfort version, left) offer a bridge between traditional and modern. The book cloth and leather have so much warmth and texture.

< 1940S FOLK ART RABBIT BOX We lucked into one of these at the 26th Street Flea Market in Chelsea in the 1990s and found a mate for it a few years later online.

∨ OSVALDO BORSANI DESK FOR TECNO Currently placed like a console behind the sofa, the desk is more easily seen in this previous arrangement, when it lived facing the bookcase.

∧ > HANS WEGNER COW HORN CHAIR This is probably the most comfortable desk chair that's not a proper ergonomic version, and it's certainly among the most beautiful. Its centered finger joint in the backrest is one of the finest examples of Danish artisanship.

∧ > GEORGE NELSON BUBBLE LAMP
Although Nelson lamps have become a
familiar modern design trope, the classic
Bubble lamp is a great hung-the-moon focal
point in tall-ceilinged rooms.

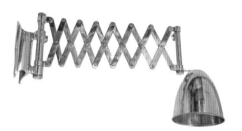

∧ ∨ NAVAL SCISSOR LAMPS Antique
brass wall-mounted scissor lamps are perfect
bedside reading lamps, even though that's not
their intended use.

∧ GUILLERME ET CHAMBRON DINING
CHAIRS We wanted to add a sculptural
modernist French element to our dining area.
These chairs have a primitive organic shape,
which is good counterprogramming to the more
delicate lines of the Danish pieces. Chris found
the set of twelve at a dealer in Paris.

∨ BISQUE PORCELAIN VASES All manner of matte white pottery goes well together. We have collected contemporary pieces by Hella Jongerius, mid-century examples by Bavarian maker Heinrich, and Rosenthal pieces like Tapio Wirkkala's Pollo bud vase.

∧ RAYMOND LOEWY SCRIPT We first discovered this tableware in an antiques store in Chicago right after we got engaged. Chris's mom bought our first set of eight or ten place settings as an engagement present. Since then, we regularly seek it out on eBay. We now have a set of seventy between Brooklyn and the beach.

∨ PIERRE FORSSELL FOR SKULTUNA We've been collecting brass objects from 1970s Swedish designer Pierre Forssell for about ten years. Our favorite find is his rocking carafe, with a rosewood stopper.

∧ CARL AUBÖCK OBJECTS Some of our most prized tabletop accessories are made by Auböck. Pictured are a horn-backed candle sconce and a carafe with a leather cuff.

∨ ANTIQUE NAPKIN RINGS We have been collecting antique silver napkin rings for about fifteen years—we always look for them at antiques stores, flea markets, and estate sales. We like to pull them out during the holidays when we host extended family so each family member can choose their own. In addition to adding a shimmer to the table, napkin rings offer a connection to history. Every once in a while, we pore over inscriptions of names and occasions—"Christmas 1861" or "Nettie 1901."

∨ MEPRA ICE ORO FLATWARE The sleek Italian design is especially elegant in the matte gold finish.

∧ BRUTALIST ART POTTERY These chunky, mid-century Danish vases offer a *jolie laide* (see page 112) quality that balances the more minimal furnishings.

∨ TEAK TRAYS BY JENS QUISTGAARD FOR DANSK These are among the hardest-working items in our kitchen. We have a standing Friday-night movie and take-out sushi ritual in our upstairs den. It's the one meal a week we don't eat in the kitchen or dining room. So for the past seventeen years, we've used the trays to transport all manner of dishes, beverages, and dipping sauces. The best part: the inset handles that allow them to hang, thus freeing up valuable cupboard space.

∧ LIBECO LINENS As far as new linen goes, we love Libeco's shorter runners. We lay them crosswise as a more modern take on place mats. We also collect antique French and Belgian mangle cloths (the layer of fabric that protected clothing in a rotary iron), with their signature red, orange, or blue stripes, to use as long table runners.

Decorating by Mood

ALL DESIGN IS MORE INTERESTING WHEN IT'S NOT ONE-NOTE. As every fashion stylist and editor knows, great personal style comes from a mix of influences, price points, degrees of formality, shapes, proportions, and so on.

Just as it's a snore to see someone wear a single designer from head to toe (a "full look" in fashion world parlance), a room that's all one era, movement, or retailer isn't revealing anything about its inhabitants' tastes. It's the problem that mid-century modern ran into in the early 2000s— every TV commercial that wanted to convey "hip young family" had some version of this trio: Eames chair, Knoll coffee table, flokati rug. These design elements, all perfectly interesting in their own right, became tired when they weren't mixed in with other periods and styles.

Our advice, and our challenge to you as you design your space, is this: Don't worry about sticking to a single country of origin, or decade, or artistic movement. Think instead about mood. Vibe. Feeling. A room that combines an organic-shaped chair with a travertine console creates a rich and warm sensibility, regardless of whether either piece is 1940s French or 1960s Brazilian. We've identified five moods here: Clean, Romantic, Earthy, Sexy, and Jolie Laide. And we've selected ten pieces that we think capture each one. Note that not all moods are as versatile as others—we find that a space can handle a *lot* of Clean and Romantic elements, for example, but more than a touch of Sexy can send you into an '80s flashback.

All this adds up to countless possible combinations in any room or throughout your home. Mix and match with abandon, and most important, have some fun doing it.

CLEAN

SO MUCH OF OUR SENSIBILITY FALLS INTO THIS MOOD.
"Clean," to us, means simple forms; honest, natural materials; and pale
fabrics and finishes. It evokes the soap-finish oak chairs of Hans Wegner,
and Pierre Chapo's elm bookcases. The shearling lounge chairs of Flemming
Lassen, and the untanned leather of a Børge Mogensen Hunting chair.

    Clean also dovetails with the movement around hygge, the Danish
quality of comfort—which, don't be fooled, is more about hard surfaces
with sheepskin pelts than a La-Z-Boy. The beech and linen campaign
furniture from Ole Gjerløv-Knudsen might sum this up perfectly: brilliantly
portable (in fact, it comes with its own carry bag) and made entirely without
metal hardware (it's tension fitted with sisal rope), it's either the most
comfortable camping furniture or the least comfortable home furniture.

    We love Clean because it lightens a room. And we have a pretty high
threshold for it compared with the other moods we're discussing here—but
too much Clean and you're living in IKEA. An all-Scandinavian home can
look stark and cold. But when mixed with darker tones (Sexy) or heavier
antiques (Romantic), Clean gives the room a necessary spareness.

1.

2.

3.

4.

5.

6.

1. Axel Einar Hjorth's Utö table represents elemental shapes at their best: a trunk base topped with a sturdy round top.
2. Flemming Lassen's classic Scandinavian armchair pairs 1940s curves with plush sheepskin. 3. Arne Jacobsen's Series 7 chair, with arms and casters, is about as minimal as an office chair gets. 4. Reminiscent of a church pew, Rainer Daumiller's 1970s pine Swedish bench mixes traditional and modern.
5. This brass and teak bench by Finn Juhl can double as a coffee table or seating (with a thin cushion). 6. With its thick shelves and beautiful corner joinery, Pierre Chapo's bookcase in elm is an exercise in humility and utility. 7. The oft-copied Luxus mirror by Uno & Östen Kristiansson hangs by a simple leather strap. 8. This beautifully crafted Hans Wegner desk shows his mastery of subtle details, like a rounded edge and inset keyholes. 9. Børge Mogensen's Hunting chair is a lower-slung take on his Spanish chair—both are surprisingly comfortable.
10. With its organic shape and sheepskin upholstery, Finn Juhl's Pelican chair is a sculptural cocoon.

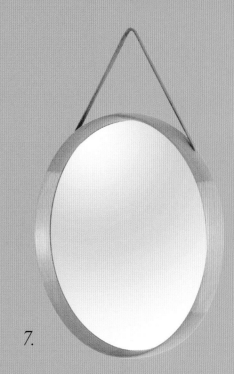

7.

8.

9.

10.

ROMANTIC

NOW, PERHAPS A SINUOUSLY CARVED HANDLE ON A WALL-
hung vanity isn't everyone's idea of romance. But there is something
sensuous, if not sensual, in the finer details of furniture design, like the
leggy profile of a Silvio Cavatorta mirrored credenza or the corseted back
of a René Gabriel oak armchair. This overt nod to femininity is, not
coincidentally, a kinship with older antiques—the painted Flora cabinet by
Josef Frank is as joyful as its rococo forebearers.

On the subject of antiques: Our sensibility is primarily modern, whether
strict modernism or jazzy deco. But the judicious addition of antique
furniture is *everything*. These pieces show your confidence in mixing genres
and periods, and they set a context for the eye to view modern design with
more clarity and appreciation. Interior architect Thomas O'Brien (see
page 236) is a maestro in this area. He made us see the Chippendale chair
in an entirely new light by pairing it with a sleek chromed aluminum and
walnut table in his Manhattan apartment. Closer to home, Pilar's carved,
English high-backed bench has mixed well in every home we've had, with
Saarinen tulip tables and Tibetan carpets alike.

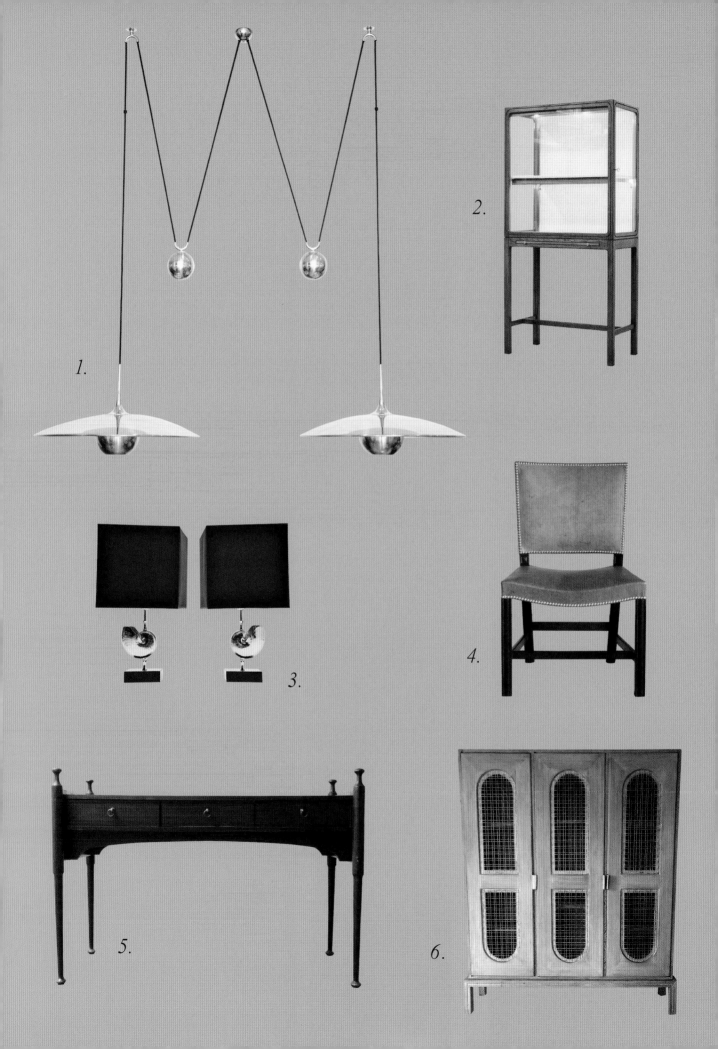

1.

2.

3.

4.

5.

6.

1. Florian Schulz's Onos lamp is jewelry-like in its mirror finish and finely detailed fittings. 2. A 1940s display cabinet in the style of Carl-Axel Acking balances elegant simplicity with fine craftsmanship. 3. A pair of gilt nautilus shell lamps with square shades showcases a successful push-pull between organic and refined, feminine and masculine. 4. An early example of Danish modernism from the 1920s, Kaare Klint's iconic Red chair is shown here in Cuban mahogany and leather. 5. A delicate mid-century three-drawer desk in mahogany nods to Jean Royère's Quilles dressing table. 6. A Tommi Parzinger tall cabinet marries limed oak with open weave caning. 7. Tall enough to protect against outgoing sparks and incoming wayward children, a nineteenth-century fireplace fender, often called a nursery guard, sits delicately on brass ball feet. 8. The spare articulating brass wall lamp by Maison Lunel is topped with a traditional shade. 9. Bernt Petersen's rosewood stool from the 1950s defines elegant with its delicate legs and caned seat. 10. Klint's Addition sofa combines buttoned tufting and modern lightness of form, providing an easy bridge between various design periods.

7.

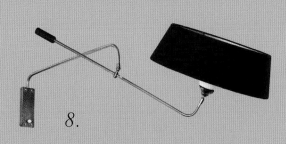

8.

9.

10.

EARTHY

THE EASIEST INTERPRETATION OF THIS MOOD MIGHT BE THE live-edge tables and benches of the master of wood, George Nakashima, which live up to his mantra to release the "soul of the tree." But "earthy" can also describe Isamu Noguchi's Akari paper lamps, which are like the moon incarnate, adding a soft glow to any room. And we think even the modernist French 1950s designs can be found in this mood—such as Pierre Chapo's Œil table with its funky god's-eye quality, and Pierre Jeanneret's Kangaroo chair, which just feels groovier than other hunting-chair styles of the period. We also like to use items from nature as accent pieces. Interesting river rocks, shells and coral, hunks of burled wood—in their own way, and mixed with machined objects, they all read as modern design. Best of all, they can't be improved upon in their organic state.

Earthy (this pun is unavoidable) just *grounds* a room. But too much and you're in Big Sur, California. While some people's idea of heaven is the Post Ranch Inn, we feel the overuse of organic form and hand-wrought texture veers a little too far into yarn crafts and driftwood furniture territory. But incorporate just enough and you have a nice balance to sleeker design and a wonderfully nature-based honesty within a modern interior.

1.

2.

3.

4.

5.

6.

7.

1. Poul Kjærholm's sinuous PK24 wicker chaise looks almost like a bird in flight. **2.** Warm and sturdy, this pine dining set by Rainer Daumiller seems suitable for a family of bears. **3.** George Nakashima's much imitated live-edge walnut coffee table with butterfly joints is the ultimate homage to natural beauty. **4.** Eero Saarinen's Tulip table, with veined marble and sculptural pedestal base, is irreducible and organic. **5.** With a bridle leather seat, this easily collapsible and versatile Egyptian stool by Danish designer Ole Wanscher was inspired by his travels to the temple of Thebes and his fascination with seats of power. **6.** Carl Auböck's leather and brass serving tray just gets better with age. **7.** Ubald Klug's Terrazza sofa is a veritable topography in leather. **8.** Characterized by washi paper made from the bark of the mulberry tree, Isamu Noguchi's handmade Akari lamps combine Japanese handicraft with modern sculptural form. **9.** These 1960s craft oak stools look as if they're about to amble off. **10.** A brutalist French oak chair from the 1940s marries organic curves with simple solidity.

8.

9.

10.

SEXY

WHAT DO WE MEAN BY SEXY? LOUCHE, NAUGHTY, A BIT
dangerous even. Perhaps the most iconic Sexy space was the fashion
designer Halston's New York City home—all black leather, shiny surfaces,
and precipitous ledges. On some level, when we say "sexy," we're
hearkening to this disco-into-yuppie era, starting somewhere with Yves
Saint Laurent (and his designer François Catroux) in 1970s Paris and ending
with Patrick Bateman and his *American Psycho* Manhattan of the 1980s.
We're thinking of chrome and smoked-glass tables, suede modular couches,
the swingy home bars by Willy Rizzo—basically a big, illicit party.

    We love this mood because it adds a little danger to the mix and
hardens the soft edges of much of our aesthetic. Almost without exception,
what we think of as sexy furniture was highly out of favor for decades.
And some examples, like vintage brass and glass cocktail tables, are still
fairly cheap and plentiful. But much of it has enjoyed a crush of demand in
the past few years. Credit the Italians for generating a lot of this heat: The
early pieces by Italian makers B&B Italia and Cassina, like designer Tobia
Scarpa's Soriana sofa and Mario Bellini's Camaleonda sofa, have recently
been reissued because of the astronomical prices the vintage pieces fetch.
Pieces by Gabriella Crespi, Gae Aulenti, Angelo Mangiarotti, and others are
the equally pricey go-tos for jet-setters wanting to add a sense of glamour to
their spaces. Our word of caution: Add Sexy to your home in moderation.
Too much and your friends might start worrying about you.

1.

2.

3.

4.

5.

6.

7.

1. Piet Hein's 1976 designs, with their sleek chrome bases and supple leather seats, are the stilettos of barstools. 2. Tobia Scarpa's low, loungy leather sofa with chrome supports is a bad-boy riff on the gentleman's club tufted banquette. 3. The name of Pierre Paulin's Groovy chair speaks for itself. 4. Roberto Menghi's Libra-Lux brass lamps are counterweighted to perch on the side of a table. 5. A contemporary of Scarpa, Mario Bellini designed the Bambole sofa for B&B Italia in 1972. 6. A mushroom lamp by German company Hillebrand comes in brass or chrome, with various shade materials and colors. 7. The Serpentine sofa by Vladimir Kagan certainly invites lounging, if not loucheness. 8. Fabio Lenci's glass and leather Hyaline chair is a feat of engineering as much as design—the tubular seat supports appear to float. 9. Poul Kjærholm's PK80 daybed is the quintessentially sexy side of Danish design, with a minimal, angular steel base. 10. Angelo Mangiarotti's signature tension-fit Eros table locks the base and top with gravity and balance alone.

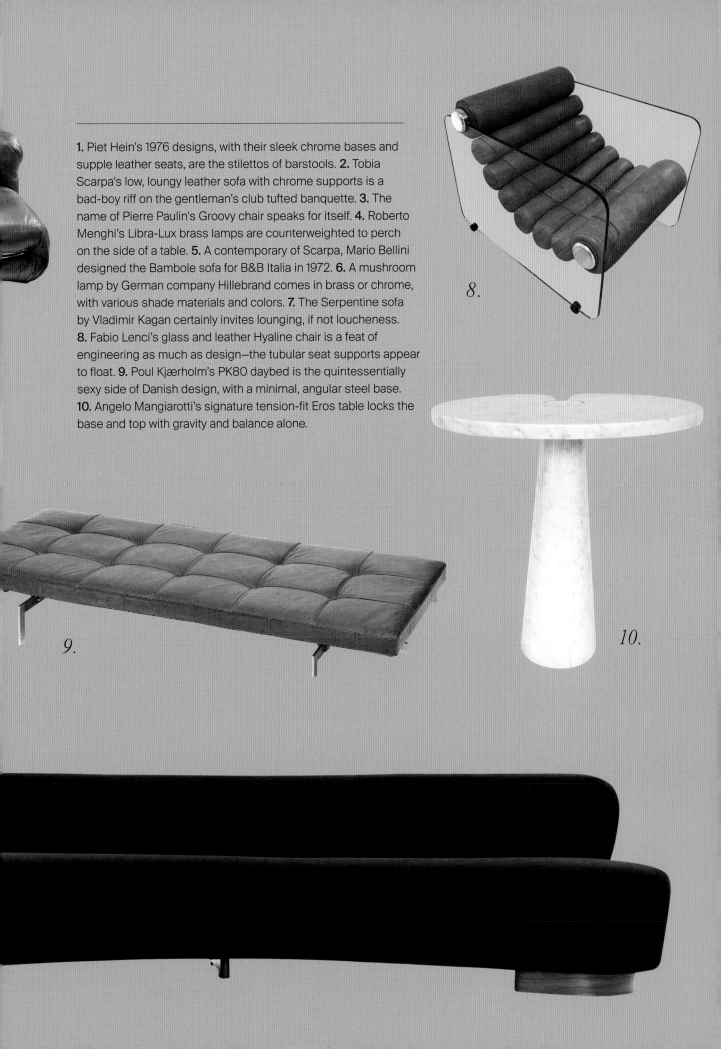

8.

9.

10.

JOLIE LAIDE

PLAYFUL, QUIRKY, EVEN A LITTLE AWKWARD: IN FRENCH, THE
phrase *jolie laide* (which translates as "pretty ugly") is used to describe
someone whose overall face is appealing even if their individual features
aren't. It might seem strange to advocate for anything that can veer into
ugly, but we have come to love things that add a little weirdness to the mix.
There's a great adage by the architecture critic Paul Goldberger that humor
doesn't work in architecture because the joke gets old and the building
remains. And as of this writing, there is a wave of ironic maximalism in
design circles that we think has already gotten stale. But we still tend to
agree with designer Jacques Grange, who said about furnishings, "I find a
certain absence of ugliness far worse than ugliness."

   The right *jolie laide* pieces can add so much character to a room that they
jar us out of our polite decorum. The Jangada chair, by Brazilian designer
Jean Gillon, with its knotted seat support and floppy leather cushions, looks
more like a spider than a lounger. And the brutalist Swedish pottery of the
1970s, with its rough, lumpy, lavalike texture (sometimes with rope and chain
for handles—see page 115), hits a chunky note that looks really nice against
the refined or delicate.

   Jolie Laide is also whimsy: Guillerme et Chambron designed credenzas
in postwar France that had built-in lamps, like a streetlight growing out
of the side of a cabinet. The pop-art Cactus coatrack by Guido Drocco
and Franco Mello in the 1980s is literally a foam cactus. John Dickinson's
plaster Africa tables from the 1970s are positively anthropomorphic, with
their articulated toes. The trick here, we believe, is to remember that a little
of this mood goes a long way. But it's a nice idea to add some humor to
your room—sparingly.

1.

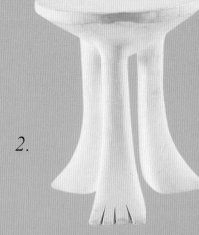

2.

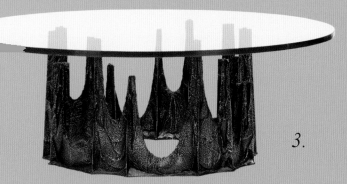

3.

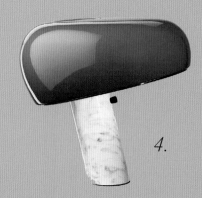

4.

5.

6.

1. A Charles Dudouyt credenza in oak features playful carved motifs throughout. 2. John Dickinson's anthropomorphic Africa table bares its toes. 3. Paul Evans was the master of metal—shown here, his aptly named Stalagmite coffee table. 4. Achille and Pier Giacomo Castiglioni's 1967 Snoopy lamp was inspired by the round snout of its beagle namesake. 5. Aldo Tura did many varieties of pedestal bars—replete with chunky hardware, and often in slightly garish shades of green, red, or yellow goatskin. 6. In the Brazilian family, Sergio Rodrigues's Tonico chair is often seen with charismatic cushions in apple-green fabric. 7. The Jean Gillon Jangada chair looks (to us, anyway) like an arachnoid. 8. A rough-textured brutalist vase is accented with heavy rope. 9. Another Paul Evans coffee table; this one, with its signature patchwork metalwork, has just the right amount of heft (and quirk) to anchor a sitting area. 10. This wall lamp from the 1950s is by Bruno Gatta, who founded the influential (and today much-copied) Italian lighting company Stilnovo.

7.

8.

9.

10.

The Galleon

"Wet bathing suits, sandy feet, and errant drinks are all part of what ensures a relaxed house, even if the Hamptons have become a very unrelaxed place since we first started spending time there."

OUR LOVE AFFAIR WITH THE EAST END OF LONG
Island began more than twenty-five years ago, and it defines
the place for us very differently from how you might think
of "the Hamptons." Our Hamptons
didn't have celebrities, nightclubs,
or high-heeled charity galas. Ours
barely had shoes.

Early on in our time in New
York, circa 1994, we lucked into a
summer rental in a house in East
Hampton Village. This was slightly
before the area became synonymous
with a haven for rich people, so we
had no preconceived ideas about
what we were getting ourselves into.

Ours was a tiny cottage, circa
1920, located half a block from
the train station. Since none of the
couples in our small group had
access to a car, we would travel by
way of the Long Island Rail Road
from New York Penn Station. In
those days, the train was still pulled
by a belching diesel locomotive, and
each car—un-air-conditioned and
unchanged from the 1950s—boasted
red vinyl seats, operable windows,
and open-air platforms where we'd sneak cigarettes.

Upon arrival, we'd walk the short distance to our
cottage, find the hide-a-key, and dispatch a few of our
members on bicycles for provisions. What followed was
pretty much the same routine every weekend: make a
charcoal fire on the grill, drag the battered dining room

table and chairs out into the backyard, and luxuriate there until dishes were cleared, wine gave way to whiskey, and bugs descended. The sum total of the technology in our one-bathroom house—with its claw-foot tub that we feared would fall into the dining room at some point, and its semi-private outdoor shower—was a rotary telephone and an aging, cassette-tape boom box.

The next morning: coffee, a pancake-and-eggs breakfast only twentysomethings would indulge in, then a 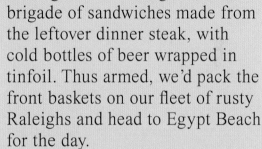 brigade of sandwiches made from the leftover dinner steak, with cold bottles of beer wrapped in tinfoil. Thus armed, we'd pack the front baskets on our fleet of rusty Raleighs and head to Egypt Beach for the day.

 Ours was a summer of bike rides on Village lanes, lazy beach reading, ragged tennis at the public courts, and too much sun. After seven summers, we realized we'd never even gone to a restaurant, with the sole exception being pizza at the local standby. If we're romanticizing that period, it's only because it remains fixed as the time and place of our salad years. Among the most idyllic of those memories was a shady street on our way to the beach, just past the Village, and just before the grand Maidstone golf club and its narrow road that spilled out to our beach. On that street, dating to the gilded-age "cottage style" of the late 1800s, were three sister houses that we counted easily as our favorites. Each looked to have been built at roughly the same time, and they all had the same squat, masculine bulk—like ships berthed on generous patches of lawn, with our most loved also having a three-

sided, third-floor dormer that reminded us of the rear cabin of an English galleon. In 2013, we discovered that this house was for sale.

We dismissed it pretty much out of hand. First, it seemed way out of our budget, even by our creative financing standards. Second, as a project, this one scared even us. Somehow we reasoned that our Brooklyn house, with neighboring houses that support one another through party walls, didn't seem like an engineering risk. But this one, noticeably listing and built on a "foundation of sand," as our then seven-year-old sagely pointed out, seemed beyond us.

But when a developer who would have razed this house backed out, we found ourselves, yet again, as the sole bidder on a dubious prize. Since we had begged and borrowed heavily, we assumed we would just live with its "charms" for a few years until we could afford a proper renovation. It would be like our old rental house, just on a ridiculously larger scale. But it quickly became clear that every good dollar we spent would be followed by many bad ones until we fixed the house's underlying structural problems. The foundation was, indeed, little more than sand, which explained why every jamb was more parallelogram than rectangle, and why all the doors had been cropped accordingly to allow them to still perform their primary function.

To correct this, we were told, the house would have to be raised about 8 feet (2.4 m) in the air while a new concrete foundation was dug and poured. After that, the house would be gently lowered onto its new base. This sounded like nothing short of a miracle to us (and to everyone we told this plan), but much in the way that an obstetrician delivers babies all day long, this was a routine operation to the house-moving company.

And that's exactly how it happened. The house went up, with hydraulic jacks and layered railroad cribs that formed giant Jenga-like piers, then small backhoes weaved in between, digging a basement level that was soon filled with concrete walls. When the house went back down, some months later, level for the first time in decades, the doorways and windows straightened themselves out, as if after a successful trip to the chiropractor.

This major step finished, we set about restoring the very wonderful bones to this house. Double-hung windows, with wavy glass and diamond panes, were stripped of their many layers of paint, revealing the fine stiles and muntins not found on today's insulated variety. A wayward broomstick revealed a series of grand ribs and coffers hidden above the suspiciously low living room ceiling. A preposterously thick Dutch front door was dismantled and rebuilt. And many more painstaking labors continued, for a period of about two years, until we were finally able to move in over a Thanksgiving weekend.

Home Tour: Little Within Big

FAR TOO MANY HOUSES IN THIS EXCLUSIVE HAMLET SEEM radically disconnected from the simple, beachy lifestyle that made the place so popular in the first place. Overstuffed rooms, fancy drapes, room upon room of wallpaper—an overall formality—make many of these "important" houses seem more appropriate to Connecticut or Park Avenue than to potato farmland by the sea. Despite having fully restored and updated a proper "cottage," we still wanted to maintain the humility of our original little rental house. The challenge was doing so with twice the square footage.

While we (thankfully) never achieved the truly spartan conditions of our 1990s rental, we did preserve the innocence of those years with our renovation. We kept technology to a minimum, and we swore to let the furniture age in ways a summerhouse demands. Wet bathing suits, sandy feet, and errant drinks are all part of what ensures a relaxed house, even if the Hamptons has become a very unrelaxed place since we first started spending time there. Here is how we tried to create a sense of charm and restraint despite a much larger footprint.

Opposite: Our sons, Willem and Henry, on a pair of Børge Mogensen Spanish chairs in the living room. Indestructible and heavily patinated, the chairs hold up to wet bathing suits and climbing kids.

THE LIVING ROOM,
AKA THE HOTEL LOBBY

The room that became the most dramatic of the house was once its least impressive. With the help of a broomstick, we discovered that a false ceiling had been added at some point, and that above it was another 2 feet (61 cm) of height (along with a grid of original structural beams and ribs). Restoring the original ceiling made the room grander, but it also brought back the correct proportion to the space, and that allowed us to treat it as multiple rooms-within-a-room. We created four distinct furniture groupings: In front of the fireplace, the linen sofa and Børge Mogensen Spanish chairs form the main sitting area. Farther back, a linen Jørgen Kastholm daybed rests under two windows that were original to the house but moved from other areas. In the lower half of the room, separated by a step, we placed a B&B Italia Charles sofa in the sunny south corner. This sits with a Danish oak coffee table and another pair of Mogensen chairs. In the final quadrant, a spare OGK daybed and an Arne Jacobsen Swan chair sit in front of a walnut sideboard by American designer William Pahlmann.

The room is large, but none of these areas is, and they enabled us to both keep the scale of the furniture small and give the areas all different (and simple) uses. One is essentially a small room to sit by the fire with cocktails. One is perfect for morning coffee and the *New York Times*. One allows for the whole family to gather around a low table and play board games. And one is centered around a discreet TV for movies on a rainy day.

Previous pages: The coffered ceiling and chair rail molding in the "hotel lobby" were original to the house and lend a heft and resolve to the millwork.

Right: A Lindsey Adelman Branching Bubble chandelier anchors the lower level of the living room. A wall of French doors leads to a bluestone patio and the pool.

Copying What's Not There

Finding the extant coffered ceiling in the living room was our great "aha" moment, but we were crushed to discover that these beams didn't carry all the way across the living room. While hardly easy, replacing the structure of the flat ceiling resulted in new beams that blend seamlessly with the original. It was a lesson to us that historical detail can be replicated to make up for any number of previous renovation sins.

Above: The B&B Italia Charles sofa makes for a perfect morning reading spot.

Opposite: The walnut sideboard by William Pahlmann bridges American craft and mid-century modern sensibilities.

THE KITCHEN

Making the kitchen small wasn't among our goals. Rather, we were hoping to avoid the trappings of a "fancy" kitchen (without losing some of the luxuries we appreciate as frequent home cooks and entertainers). We wanted it to be nice, just not the typical luxury-meets-country kitchen that's so prevalent in that neck of the woods (as seen in any Nancy Meyers movie, but especially *Something's Gotta Give*). The answer was to give the room an English scullery feel. Like in the *Upstairs, Downstairs* country estates of the nineteenth century, there is a very "downstairs" quality to this kitchen. It announces itself as hardworking and low on frills, if not on quality materials.

First, we eschewed any upper cabinets, instead running a long bank of oak drawers along the wall, modeled on an old general store. And we built a full-height oak display cabinet on the north wall. (This also helped solve for the thin wall that separates the kitchen from the dining room. We didn't like its partition quality, so building up some depth gave the necessary bulk to that division.) For shine, we developed a custom-colored ceramic tile in a creamy white for the whole room, lending it a kind of hose-it-down quality that definitely screams utility of purpose. To recess the fridge, we stole space from an overly large powder room on the other side. In the middle is a quintessential worktable: shallow drawers, open shelves underneath, and chamfered legs.

Leading with a Narrative

One of the things we most feared when embarking on this project was having any newly reworked rooms feel suburban. For example, we were sensitive to having seen too many Hamptons kitchens with the same layout of upper cabinets, large vent hood, and refrigerator cabinet. We wanted our kitchen to have a specific sense of time and place. Our inspiration was from the nineteenth-century English manor houses: fully tiled walls, oak drawers, and a massive worktable all give the room a sense of utilitarian purpose and nod to the grand kitchens of *Downton Abbey* and *The Remains of the Day*.

Opposite: A sunken china cabinet backed in the same subway tile as the walls provides a museum-like display for glassware and china. Glass shelves and interior lights let this cabinet glow in the evenings.

Following pages: The rough-hewn ceiling beams were in the house when we bought it, and they add warmth and imperfection to the kitchen. We paired them with small Edison lights instead of more typical recessed lighting.

THE BREAKFAST ROOM

One of our abiding joys is having a kitchen full of people while the meal is being prepared, and so we added a space off the kitchen for that purpose. Lower by a step, the "breakfast room" becomes a real room of its own, a kind of reverse observation deck onto the activity of the kitchen. Borrowing from our Brooklyn banquette (see page 54), we supersized one for this room, where eight or so people can gather with a glass while Pilar and friends cook. The leather Pot chair is by Arne Jacobsen. We used a marble table by Eero Saarinen and a set of French metal Tolix chairs to create a second, more casual dining area. A pair of wonderfully imperfect Lindsey Adelman Knotty Bubbles pendants provides a nice glow overhead and connects the two furniture groupings.

Left: We like the interplay of patterns between the antique Cossack rug from Pilar's childhood home and the exploded floral of the BDDW Harroll rug.

THE DINING ROOM

One of the benefits of an old house is that many
of the rooms have modest proportions for heat
retention. This original dining room is quite small
given the size of the house, but it's perfect for
creating intimacy. It also offers the nicest midday
light in all seasons, and thus is our favorite place
to gather for a long lunch. In colder months, we
make ample use of the fireplace, which doubles
the coziness. Accents of black, in the David Weeks
chandelier and leather Series 7 armchairs by Arne
Jacobsen, give a graphic counterpoint to the oak
table, Lapland sheepskin throws, and English
sandstone fireplace mantel.

Getting the Proportions Right

The charm of old houses resides in the scale and proportions
of the rooms. Some, like the living room, are fairly grand and
speak to their original use as a parlor for multiple activities.
But compared with today's construction, most of the rooms
in these turn-of-the-last-century houses are surprisingly
modest, given the overall size of the buildings themselves.
This restraint speaks to the way people actually lived in
these seasonal homes, where entertaining wasn't usually on
a lavish scale the way it might be in grand New York City
apartments or in the Gold Coast estates of Long Island.
As such, the dining room here retains a coziness precisely
because it isn't huge. This is a lesson we've learned to adopt
when designing an addition or rethinking the layout of an
existing house. We find, and we're probably not alone, that
our initial instinct is to go as big as we can. But it's precisely
when we've scaled back the dimensions of a room, or
narrowed a doorway, or reduced a window size, that we've
captured an intimacy that makes the space so much more
charming and special.

Above: The English sandstone mantel is by London-based Jamb. With the fireplace and the oak table reinforcing the neutrals in the dining room, we added black accents in the chairs and chandelier to punctuate the space (one of our signature loyalties is to the color black—see page 40).

THE PRIMARY BEDROOM

The primary bedroom suite is the only one that
runs the full depth of the house, enjoying a view
in the back to the pool and a commanding vantage
in the front onto a majestic copper beech tree.
This room proved another lesson in proportion
for us: we retained the modest size of the original
bedroom (now the sleeping area), but joined it via
a passageway to an adjoining dressing room and
lounge/office.

Previous pages: Original leaded-glass
windows and nineteenth-century Austrian
mounts fill a wall of the two-story stairwell. A
redwood table made by Pilar's grandfather
provides a place for books on the landing.

Right: The Hans Wegner teak and brass
daybed is upholstered in an ivory wool bouclé.
The teak dresser is by Hvidt & Mølgaard, and
the snake block print is by Seattle artist (and
friend of ours) Jen Ament.

Following pages: An earlier arrangement
of the primary bedroom. The RH bed is
dressed in Libeco linens. The 1950s safari
chair is by Wilhelm Kienzle, and the vintage
counterbalanced lamp by Édouard-Wilfred
Buquet sits on an Eero Saarinen side table.
Another Ament piece, a block print feather,
hangs over the dresser.

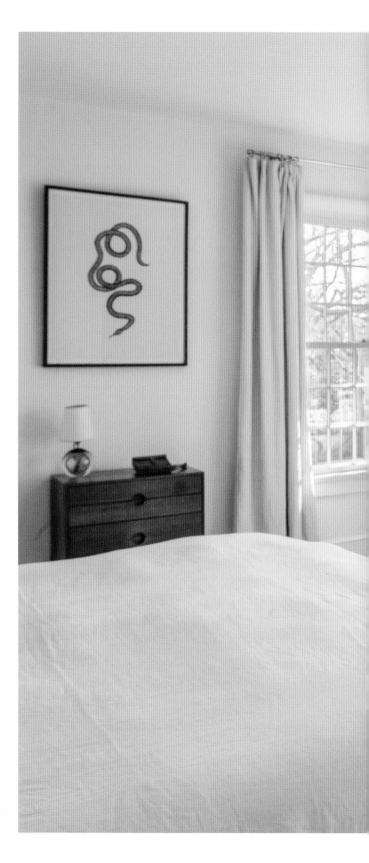

THE DRESSING ROOM

This dressing room was originally a separate den with a TV (following our Brooklyn tradition of not having a television in the first-floor public spaces). But when we added a basement game room, the upstairs den went largely unused, so we combined the two adjacent rooms. The wall of custom oak closets and drawers gave us much-needed storage, as well as a gracious new entrance when we sealed off the original door into the bedroom. The result is a private, sun-filled aerie with wraparound exposures.

Left: The primary bedroom leads via a wide passageway to the adjoining dressing room and lounge. The vintage leather daybed is by Poul Kjærholm.

THE PRIMARY BATH

In refashioning the rear elevation of the East
Hampton house, we created a larger terrace off the
primary bathroom. The ability to lounge there after
a bath, or with a morning cup of coffee, epitomizes
the lazy enjoyment of summer for us. We used small
Carrara brick for all the walls, creating a uniform
palette for white pedestal sinks and a bateau tub.

Modernizing Traditional Tile

Floor-to-ceiling tile adds real drama. We
found this to be true in both the kitchen and
the bathrooms, where tile gave the rooms a
combination of practical (the illusion that the
whole space could be hosed down) and luxe.
Most historic baths ended wall tile at a chair-
rail. And many newer builds copy that lower
height for cost effectiveness, but with higher
runs of tile in the shower area. Extending
the wall tile to the ceiling may be a bit more
expensive, but it eliminates the jog in height
between the shower and the rest of the bathroom
that we've always found to be a jarring.

Right: The primary bath has a cast-iron bateau
tub by Barclay and a rosewood Butterfly stool
by Sori Yanagi.

THE FRENCH HOSPITAL

On the third floor, a vestige of turn-of-the-nineteenth-century houses that is no longer permitted under the current building code, we wanted rooms for the kids (and visiting kids) that would feel like their own camp. And because the dormers created a jumble of angles and corners, we covered walls and ceilings alike in crisp, white wainscoting. When we were done, the largest of the rooms on this floor, the one boasting our adored three-sided, diamond-paned dormer, felt like a French hospital from the World War I era. Somewhere between that influence and a Maine camp are the lined-up rows of twin beds, Ralph Lauren swing-arm lamps, and Pendleton blankets. It's a room with purpose, simplicity, and charm.

Left: The three-sided window in the beadboard-lined bunk is what first drew us to this house many years before. We placed a desk in the window bay to inspire daydreaming, if not letter writing. The quartet of oak beds are by Muji, and the bronze wall lamps are by Ralph Lauren.

THE CARRIAGE HOUSE

While we renovated the house, an old garage
remained as is, storing the ever-expanding
collection of furniture that would eventually
populate the main house. Once we were done, we
turned our attention to this equally old if historically
less-loved structure. We rebuilt and reshingled it,
restoring the original carriage house doors and
the two large, mullioned picture windows. And we
added a pergola off the side, planted with wisteria
that climbs up the posts. The result is a bit of
Provence in the Hamptons—a fragrant, shaded
place to enjoy long lunches. A bank of French doors
leads inside, where we clad the walls in simple
cedar planks and laid a rough-hewn barnwood floor.
The space does double duty as an indoor-outdoor
living area and place to stow our 1965 Jeep.

Right: Hydrangeas, boxwood hedges, and
lavender bushes help turn an erstwhile garage
into a dining pavilion/patio.

Above: New sets of French doors open the carriage house to the dining pavilion and pergola and look onto the backyard pool area and rear side of the house (which is arguably the most beautiful).

Opposite: Salvaged diamond-paned doors provide a newly created egress off the main house. The bed is filled with clipped boxwoods, hydrangeas, and lavender—all classic Hamptons plant materials.

Design Notes

< ∧ RUSH-HANDLED BASKETS We use these baskets from Pottery Barn (the largest size is best) for everything from firewood to beach towels.

∧ CABLE-KNIT BLANKETS Cashmere throws are a weakness of ours, in part because they offer such an easy added layer of decorating. This one is by Ralph Lauren Home.

∧ ILLUM WIKKELSØ PLEXUS OAK AND CANE
CHAIRS Oak and cane always make a winning
combination. The traditional materials, when reimagined in
a modern silhouette, take on either a 1970s or tropical vibe.
The Plexus series, designed in the 1960s, was conceived
to be totally modular—the caned sides and backs can be
configured for sofas or chairs.

∧ LINDSEY ADELMAN
KNOTTY BUBBLES
CHANDELIER Made of hand-
blown glass and tied together
with knotted rope, these
barnacle-like fixtures—part of
Adelman's Roll & Hill Knotty
Bubbles series—are inspired by
Japanese buoys.

< JOHN DERIAN FIELD BENCH
This low-back sofa in oatmeal
linen, with its deep-buttoned tufting
and lengthy proportions, bridges
traditional and contemporary styles.
While okay for occasional seating,
this isn't a sink-in-and-watch-a-movie
comfort piece. Its best use is under
windows, which tend to be low in
older cottage-style houses.

> LINDSEY ADELMAN BRANCHING
BUBBLE CHANDELIER Like a Cartier
Love bracelet, Adelman's beautiful chandelier
is ubiquitous for a reason. With its irregular
handblown glass globes, it is at once elegant
and organic.

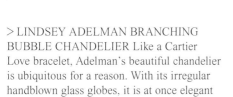

> GOTLAND SHEEPSKINS While you can get
sheepskins in a lot of places, including IKEA, we tend to
favor ones from Gotland, the largest island off Sweden.
Sheep have been grazing on this sparse island since
the 1970s, and their years of breeding have produced
beautiful lambskins with silky curls in all different
shades of mottled gray, from taupes to charcoals. They
are a little more expensive than other options, but they're
worth it: Gotland sheepskins don't become matted or
felted, thanks to the high quality of the fur. And the
sheep are sustainably and humanely raised.

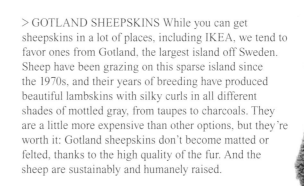

< BDDW TRIPOD LAMP Both
totemic and warm, the BDDW
tripod lamp can anchor an entire
corner of a room, much like a
sculptural chair would.

> SERIES 7 ARNE JACOBSEN CHAIRS
The Series 7 may be the most-copied chair
of all mid-century classics (it's in stiff
competition with the Wishbone chair).
The armchair has a complexity lacking in
the original armless version, and leather
upholstery adds a comfort level the laminated
wood lacks. There's even a version with
casters, which is perhaps our all-time favorite.
In our dining room set, we like the push-pull
of the sleek black silhouette against the hygge
vibes of the sheepskin.

∨ BUTTERFLY STOOL Designed in 1954 by Sori Yanagi, this ingeniously simple stool is made of two identical bentwood pieces that are fastened by brass bolts and a center tension rod.

< RALPH LAUREN WESTBURY SCONCE The horse-bit detail of this brass and mirror sconce gives it an equestrian feeling.

> BLACK FOREST MOUNTS We are neither Bavarians nor hunters, but we love the stark graphic minimalism of these tiny nineteenth-century antler mounts when they're hung en masse on a stark white wall.

∨ > ARNOLD MADSEN CLAM CHAIR The provenance of this sheepskin chair, which has seen its value skyrocket in recent years, has been the subject of a minor controversy. Long credited to Danish designer Philip Arctander, it was recently reattributed to fellow Dane Arnold Madsen.

∧ ARNE JACOBSEN POT CHAIR This chair—
which is a sister to our first love, the Swan chair
(see page 63)—stands out for its almost childlike
modern silhouette. There's something about the
juxtaposition of the modern shape with a patinated
vegetable-dyed leather that almost feels like an old
baseball glove. You can anchor a corner of a room
with little else.

∧ KAARE KLINT SAFARI CHAIRS We love the
simplicity of these endlessly movable campaign chairs.
They are easy to buy online—and pack flat so you can
stash them in the overhead bin of an airplane if you
happen to find them in Denmark. While we favor the
oak and leather versions, they come in oak and canvas
as well. Given their simple design, they are another
wonderful bridge of modern and traditional styles.

∧ RÖRSTRAND BLÅ ELD (BLUE FIRE)
HERRINGBONE PATTERN PORCELAIN These
slip-cast earthenware pieces with a subtly molded
herringbone pattern are inspired by Chinese and
Dutch porcelain. They are hard to find in complete
sets, which is why we've collected them piecemeal.
We mainly use them when serving to vary our
mostly white table settings.

< ∧ BELGIAN FOOTED BOWLS We found
these at the cult shop Ruby Beets in Sag Harbor.
We bought every one they had after the owners
told us they were no longer being made because
the original factory had burned down.

> THOMAS O'BRIEN LONG BOX SCONCES We love to use these to flank doorways because of their dramatic shape and soft light. The first place we saw them was in the bar at Ken Aretksy's Patroon, an iconic New York steak house. These lights made that room feel like a classic era train car.

∧ BREAD BOARDS We like to mix new and antique cutting boards, both as a display and for everyday use. Some new favorites are by Edward Wohl and M. Crow.

∧ > BAR CARTS Often, bar carts are too kitschy for us (probably a nod to the era in which bar carts were a thing). So when we find them in oak, and particularly in more rustic designs, we pounce. Pictured here are an English design from the 1920s (above) and a French cart from the 1930s (right).

Putting It All Together

YOU'VE BASED YOUR DESIGN ON A FEW KEY MATERIALS AND colors. And you've found the vibe you want for your various spaces. Now what? It's easy to feel paralyzed when the time comes to turn a procession of choices into an actual room. Deciding what to buy and collect, what to discard, and how to lay it all out is the purview of many a self-help organizational guru. We, too, believe that your stuff should "spark joy," as Marie Kondo puts it. Our addendum would be that things spark joy at different times of your life, and often in different arrangements.

Like the materials—oak, brass, and leather—discussed in our first lesson (see page 24), we believe rooms themselves should also get better with age. There's something liberating about accepting that there is no end to the process of creating interiors. They often need a "second layer" that can't be achieved on day one. This depth and dimension only come from the life you play out in these rooms: objects collected over time on your travels, wear and tear from parties and children, rejiggering based on the evolving needs and desires of how you use the space.

And so we like to think of decorating not so much in the old-fashioned sense of a commitment to some of-the-moment design scheme a decorator talks you into, but as a practice—one that evolves over time.

Collecting

OUR DESIGN PROCESS HAS ALWAYS BEEN INFORMED BY A LOVE
of collecting. When we were first living together and figuring out how to
merge our tastes, we began buying vintage and antique furniture. Thanks
to a friend, we fell early and hard for Danish modern, beginning a now
twenty-year-strong love affair with the craftsmanship and art of the best
Danish designers and cabinetmakers. Back then, our resources were the
few books we could find—Noritsugu Oda's *Danish Chairs* was a particularly
helpful reference. And we learned from a few amazing New York dealers,
like Modernlink's William Lee, who I'm sure gave away twice as much
knowledge as furniture he sold us. We went to shows at the Pier and the
Armory when they came to town. We also traveled to Denmark, Paris,
Madrid, and Milan, looking more than buying, but getting a feel for the
movements and schools of modern design. All of it was a gradual building of
knowledge and passion.

Discovering 1stDibs was a revelation for us. I'm sure we couldn't claim
to be early adopters, but once we found this e-commerce site that aggregates
the best vintage and antiques dealers from around the world, our collecting
went into overdrive. We use the site as much as a resource as we do a place
to buy. That's not to say we haven't shopped liberally! But equally if not
more valuable for us has been the rabbit hole of discovery that 1stDibs has
provided. Our Danish obsession led us to dealers who also had mid-century
French pieces, and we swooned for Pierre Chapo and his contemporaries.
That led to the Brazilians—funky, arachnoid chairs by Jean Gillon and the
totemic thrones of Sergio Rodrigues. Oh, and of course Italian modern—the
elegant whimsy of Ignazio Gardella's brass-footed chairs and bookshelves,
the louche sexiness of Willy Rizzo's chrome and suede bars. With each new
discovery, our collective eye adapted, and we realized that they all seemed
interconnected. No internet puns intended, but it revealed itself to us to be a
web—every era and region informing one another, sharing cultural vibes and
folk influences and moods.

It's why we focus so much here on the interplay among designers of
different countries and decades. Following this "web" gave us the education
and, in turn, the confidence to put Swedish pottery with an English settee,
or mix German 1980s with French 1930s. And far more than the individual
pieces we choose, it's that mix that informs our sensibility.

10 TIPS FOR THE NEW COLLECTOR

Collecting can be intimidating because it implies both a need for expertise and a risk of making mistakes. But if you buy with your heart and follow these simple guidelines, you'll end up with pieces that will enable you to create an infinite number of room configurations.

1 INVEST IN WELL-MADE ANCHOR PIECES.

Collect to hold, and spend accordingly—if it's an heirloom piece you'll pass down to the next generation, it will be worth the investment, and you'll get a lifetime of value from it. Pieces like credenzas and cabinets are where the quality really shows. Fine materials like book-matched rosewood and details like dovetailed drawers, inlaid corners, and carved handles are hallmarks of these pieces, and make them well worth the price.

2 SHOP WHEN YOU TRAVEL.

The Paris flea market (Marché Paul Bert, off rue des Rosiers, is the especially good section to hunt) offers shippers on-site who can send pieces overseas for less than you might think, and the savings of buying a piece abroad (and the chance to find something one of a kind) makes it usually well worth the extra hassle of shipping. In other locales, antiques dealers almost always have shipping arrangements, thanks in part to the widespread online buying community.

3 DON'T BE PUT OFF BY SMALL REPAIRS.

Easily repaired flaws (a bit of veneer loss on a cabinet, a crack in a chair, a busted caned seat) yield much better prices on otherwise beautiful pieces. While some of this fine repair is a dying art, most cities will have a few old hands who can still do the work.

4 COLLECT AROUND ONE MATERIAL.

Sometimes it is the form rather than the authenticity that makes a collection. German bisque porcelain, for instance, or brutalist pottery, can be the basis of a new collection.

5 TREAT A SIGNATURE CHAIR LIKE A PIECE OF SCULPTURE.

Some of your furniture can be objects rather than workhorses. Delicate, uncomfortable, or impractical pieces can add a sculptural element to a room and signal a refined eye. And bought as one-offs, these can be well-priced orphans.

6 CAPITALIZE ON YOUR LEGWORK.

Whether searching auction sites like eBay or LiveAuctioneers or browsing a local yard sale, if you've done some homework on the designers and eras you like, you'll probably find unattributed examples of serious pieces. A less trained eye might mistakenly buy an unknown cabinet thinking it's by Børge Mogensen (and that's okay, too), but often you'll find pieces of real provenance because the seller just doesn't know what they have. We've found some great designer pieces just by searching for "Danish oak" or "French deco," and we've found plenty of Hans Wegner by searching for slightly misspelled versions of his name.

7 BUY THE PERENNIALLY OUT OF FAVOR.

Don't worry about what is "hot," since it will likely not always be. Conversely, don't worry if a beloved piece is out of fashion. For some reason, so-called "brown furniture," for instance, which includes darker English and American antiques, have been absolute bargains for years. Most dealers and auction houses are practically giving them away. Mixing these antiques in with other genres can yield some beautifully made and beautifully priced heirlooms. In the same vein, we aren't fans of DIY tricks—we'd much rather embrace an antique mahogany secretary as-is than paint it white and replace its hardware.

8 GO DOWN THOSE RABBIT HOLES.

Searching online for designers always leads to other pieces in the same genre. This is a wonderful way to give yourself an education on design as well as to find some less celebrated pieces that are often less expensive.

9 SNIFF OUT THE NEXT WAVE.

As your eye evolves, you'll start gravitating to periods and design trends that not everyone is feeling just yet. The wave of 1980s design was decidedly uncool . . . until it wasn't. What's next? Hard to say, but lately we are drawn to George III, Biedermeier, and Swiss mid-century design.

10 WEED OUT AS YOU COLLECT.

Editing is as much a part of collecting as acquiring. To build a great collection, you must get rid of the things that you don't love. We believe that furnishing sparely with investment pieces is far better than filling your spaces with a surfeit of "meh." Or, put another way, it's better to have a few great things, bolstered by neutral staples from CB2 and IKEA, than a lot of middle-of-the-road design. Think: If good is the enemy of great, then mediocre is the enemy of both.

Arranging

OUR BROOKLYN LIVING ROOM HAS SEEN AT LEAST THREE
different furniture arrangements over the years. The one in East Hampton
had probably six. It's not uncommon for a chair, a rug, or even a sofa to move
rooms from week to week (so much so that we're quite sure the woman who
helps clean our house feels she's being gaslit).

We have found that playing with scale and density can help a room
feel dynamic. That every room is really made up of groupings that are mini
"rooms" in themselves. That organizing objects as if you always have a bird's-
eye view can help create order from chaos. But if we've learned anything,
it's that there isn't one right way to put it all together. And even if you follow
some of our advice, and like the results, you should still change it up every
so often. The eye has to travel, in the immortal words of fashion editor Diana
Vreeland. You rotate things in order to see them with fresh eyes. That's true
for the art on your walls, and it's true for the furniture.

Plus, these rooms have to grow with you. As our children got older, a
nursery became a "cloffice"—part dressing room, part study—for Pilar, and
then evolved again, coming full circle, into an almost dorm-like bedroom for
our teen.

What follows is a lesson in putting things together, whether furniture in a
room or objects on a mantel.

SHAPES & LAYOUT

The art of arranging furniture is about imagining a bird's-eye view of the room. If you treat a room like a tablescape, you'll start to envision it as a big tableau. Triangles, squares, circles, and rectangles should be intentionally mixed and varied, so the room keeps the eye moving and avoids repetition. In all our arrangements, we like to incorporate assorted round side tables, poufs, and stools—these movable pieces are great for different gatherings and multiple conversation groupings, and serve as punctuation to the larger shapes. But they maintain more or less similar spacing between these pieces so there's a cohesiveness.

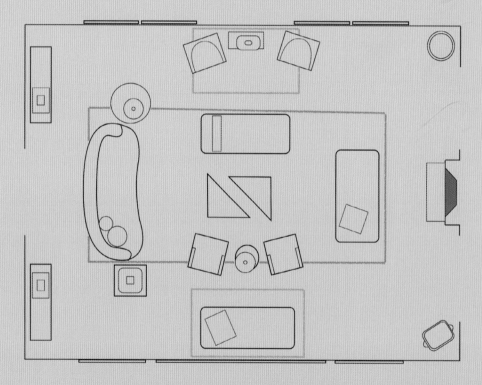

Maximize Flow:
Anchoring a Room
with a Central Core

In our Bridgehampton living room, we wanted an overall feeling of calm. We started with two triangular tables, placing them in an elongated rectangle with ample space both around and between them. A floating 9-foot (2.7 m) oval sofa grounds the center area, overlooking a rectangular daybed that protects the view of the fireplace. Another daybed and a pair of round-back chairs complete this central square. Along the sides of the room, a third low daybed allows a view out the picture window, and another pair of round-back chairs creates a tête-à-tête along the north windows. It's a varied composition of shapes that provides enough seating for a group, and it's consistently sparsely placed to let everything breathe.

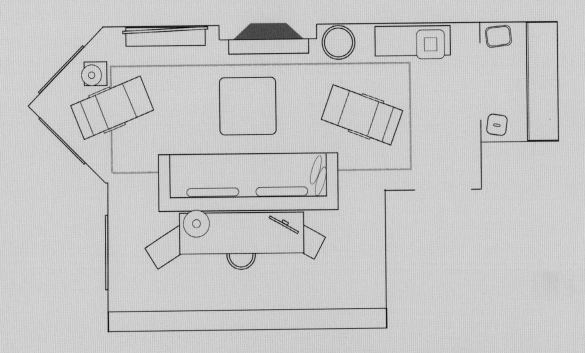

Make a Space Multitask: Using a Sofa as a Room Divider

In our Brooklyn den, we wanted the fireplace and the television to take center stage, so we anchored the middle of the room with a 90-inch (2.3 m) sofa—as big as the space would allow while still providing access on either side of it. Directly behind, a 1960s Borsani desk doubles as a console table. We placed Borsani recliners at an angle to offset the grid of rectangular shapes and mirror the angled wings of the desk. Round shapes in the form of various mushroom lamps, a Nelson Bubble lamp, and a large round mirror over the fireplace break up the rectangles.

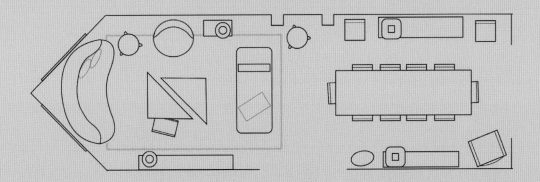

Lean into Limitations: Tricking the Eye with Novel Configurations

In our Brooklyn living room, we again began our composition with a pair of triangular coffee tables and surrounded them with an oval love seat, a round chair and stool, and rectangular pieces in the small dresser, wall cabinet, and daybed. This juxtaposition of different shapes makes for a more interesting furniture arrangement, and keeps the room from feeling narrow. A 10-foot (3 m) solid oak dining table anchors the other end of the front parlor.

DENSITY & VIGNETTES

We find that varied densities of furniture arrangements can signal different uses or feelings for areas. The sitting area of our kitchen in Brooklyn, for instance, is intentionally layered with a close arrangement of pieces. This allows a lot of people to be in this hardworking room at once, and it suggests an intimacy even when it's empty. Our Bridgehampton living room, on the other hand, was left purposely spare to create a sense of tranquility and space.

    Another one of our mantras is to think about how you're actually going to use a room. When it's going to multitask, the key is in creating separate vignettes within a single space. This can range from placing an intimate games table in the corner to sequestering a perfect armchair next to the fireplace for reading.

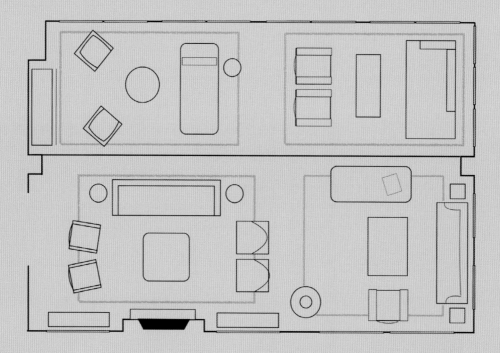

Mimic a Hotel Lounge: Creating Intimacy in Public Spaces

To break up the large space of our East Hampton living room, we created four "rooms": a sitting area in front of the fireplace, a games area in the far corner, one reading area in the windowed back corner, and another by the credenza. Each of these feels intentional and independent but also relates to the others—either with repeated signature chairs or common accessories like throws and pillows. Part of the trick is to keep enough space between areas so that each reads as an individual grouping. We find rugs go a long way to demarcate the separate areas.

3 RULES WORTH BREAKING

1 YOU CAN'T BLOCK A WINDOW.

When we made the kitchen banquette in Brooklyn, we initially worried about the sofa back partially obstructing the window on the rear wall. But the practicality of utilizing that corner prevailed, and aesthetically we came to love the layered effect (and symmetry with the island height) of cutting off that window.

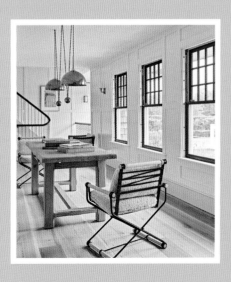

2 NARROW ROOMS CAN'T TAKE FLOATING FURNITURE.

Conventional wisdom would say that placing sofas against the side walls is space saving, but we find that it actually just closes in a narrow space. In the front parlor of our Brooklyn town house, we placed a daybed in the center of the room to mark the sitting area, but left space around it to let it breathe. That, along with a mix of floating furniture, creates an open conversation area and gives the illusion of pushing the walls outward.

3 HALLWAYS AREN'T ROOMS.

Often, hallways (particularly on the upper bedroom floors) tend to be overlooked or underloved spaces. In Bridgehampton, we expanded our second-floor landing into a wide gallery, serving as access to bedrooms and as a room of its own.

ART: PLAYING WITH PROPORTION & SCALE

One of the most-shared photos of our Brooklyn house on social media has been the back wall of our kitchen, with two large prints by Enzo Mari. We started with *Pear*, a graphic green square centered on the wall. When we came across *Apple*, we loved the idea of taking up that whole space between the windows, even though it ran contrary to normal rules of spacing. Similarly, putting large-format art on our high-ceilinged dining room and living room walls helps ground the space and keeps the furniture from looking small to scale.

    While big gestures like this can go a long way to adding depth and composition to a room, little pieces can be heroes, too. Give smaller pictures a big presence by making them a focus, or by letting them anchor a corner or an intimate seating arrangement.

STYLING OBJECTS & TABLEAUS

A key principle of ours is not to hide anything. In china cabinets, we believe that even everyday items should be beautiful, and therefore on display. As a result, we don't own separate sets of formal and everyday china—instead, we have a single set of Raymond Loewy china that is plentiful enough for everyday accidents but sufficiently elevated to use for our fanciest dinner party.

But not hiding things away requires order. A jumble of glassware isn't pleasing to look at, whether exposed or not; glasses look best when they're not only placed in like numbers but also lined up in rows. Similarly, plates and bowls should be arranged in equal-height stacks, with some rhyme and reason for their relation to one another.

Once these items are standing like soldiers, breaking the pattern adds a liveliness to the mix. Vases, decanters, and pitchers can be arranged in less orderly groupings, allowing their individuality and contrast to stand out. Finally, adding in non-kitchen items creates a museum-like quality to a china cabinet. Folded fabrics, brass and wood objects, bread boards, julep cups of flowers, even books can round out the cabinet and make it an artful tableau.

For bookshelves, similar rules apply. Rows and stacks of books should have some like-mindedness to their arrangement, but they should be broken up, and allowed to breathe, with objects both playful and sculptural. Antique toys, small lamps, sterling trays and boxes, and, of course, vases of flowers all add visual interest and varied proportion.

LIGHTING: LOW & LOTS OF IT

A room that glows feels particularly inviting. And the best way to get that vibe is with plenty of sconces and accent lamps. We pretty much avoid recessed lighting at all costs (using it only over kitchen islands, where the cook needs directed light). Instead, we place at least two sconces on each wall, and flanking almost every doorway and window. We use accent lamps to add low lighting on bookcases, fireplace mantels, and even in some cases on a credenza that already has a table lamp. We treat them as objets, kind of like candlesticks. As for bulbs, we stick to 15 to 40 watts—never higher—and even then we put dimmers on everything.

A Word About Brass Lamps

For us, there is little that has been more fun, or time-consuming, than diving down rabbit holes of vintage brass lamps. They tend to fall into three categories: maritime, mid-century Italian, and 1970s German. Maritime brass (bulkheads, scissor lamps, even table lamps made for yachts) are typically unlacquered, and always thick and heavy. Original Italian brass lamps by Stilnovo and others are increasingly hard to find, but each discovery is like a treasure—the delicate counterweights and cantilever mechanisms, the conical (and sometimes perforated) metal shades, the "Swinging Sixties meets Paris atelier" quality they possess. But our latest and most fulfilling trails have been pursuing German lamps by Hillebrand and Florian Schulz. These are what table lamps should be, and we are always surprised by the dearth of any modern manufacturing that comes close. Their mushroom shades, thick column stems, and just gorgeous precision to the milling and hardware make them exceptional finds.

Palmer Cottage

"What we needed was detail. Quirks. Artifacts.
It is hugely ironic that this, our oldest house by a hundred
years, seemed to reveal no history."

AS PRECOCIOUS KIDS, WE WERE BOTH HOME-
design geeks, predisposed to the charms of old houses.
From a young age, Chris watched *The Money Pit* (the 1980s
comedy about a pair of yuppies
whose home renovation nearly does
them in) not as a cautionary tale but
as an aspirational road map. Pilar,
raised in an improbably old house in
Los Angeles—a 1920s English Tudor
that felt more Westchester than
Beverly Hills—took it upon herself
to subscribe to *Architectural Digest*
at age eight. Perhaps that explains
why we were both so maniacal about
finding houses with good bones.

    When we were ready to try our
hand at another project on a slightly
bigger scale, the house we spied
in Bridgehampton seemed like the
perfect specimen—a Slim Aarons
photo, missing only the handsome
family posed out front. In reality,
it was more like the backlot of a
Hollywood studio, whose houses are
just facades propped up from behind
by scaffolding.

    Built in 1700, this house was
the original farmhouse on our small lane. It was renovated
thoroughly—and, we imagine, well—in 1902 by a couple
who gave it its lasting moniker, Palmer Cottage. And it
sat happily for eighty-five years as a shingle-style cottage,
albeit with the low-ceilinged frame that gave away its earlier
origins.

The longtime owners before us were great stewards of the estate in so many ways, from building the clay tennis court to facilitating legendary summer parties where actor John Belushi apparently consumed illegal substances on the pool coping and the aerialist Philippe Petit once walked the roofline. So we don't hold anything against them that they chose to undergo a full interior renovation in 1987, at the nadir of 1980s sensibility. (This was a terrible decade for traditional architecture, a time when the yuppie appreciation of all things luxury brought back a lot of period detail, but in cheap substitutes: think hollow-core doors, vinyl windows, and prefinished wood floors.)

By the time we came along, in 2018, all that remained of the 1902 renovation was the pretty roofline that arced gently at the corners, over deep eaves. Which meant that taking on this project necessitated rethinking our approach to renovation. Up to this point, we had restored only houses with good bones, in part because that's what we had been handed. We had always taken pride in our ingenuity, in our ability to find an elegant solution to a problem. To piece back together the inevitably incomplete puzzle. That's the essence of restoration; the restrictions are your freedom.

Designing, on the other hand, is a blank canvas, and applying those first strokes was definitely daunting. Committing to a course of action has the obvious downside of what economists call opportunity risk. By choosing one path, you close another. What if you regret your indelible mark? But not choosing is its own quagmire. In renovations, this problem results in houses we call "window catalogs," when homeowners add a few Palladians, and an oculus or two, because it's just so hard to choose. The trick, perhaps, is forcing restraint. Coco Chanel's famous line, "Before you leave the house, look in the mirror and take one thing off," applies equally to design. In architecture, as in life, the tyranny of choice is best tempered by the clarity of conviction.

With Palmer Cottage, what we had was a classic, shingle-style shape. What we needed was detail. Quirks. Artifacts. It is hugely ironic that this, our oldest house by a hundred years, seemed to reveal no history. No hints of gracious expansions over the centuries.

So that's where we started— with some invented history. We opted to shift the house's location, to give it a bit more breathing room from the tennis court. Then we set about trying to expand it— thoughtfully, with its own backstory. The new wood banding that wraps the totality of the dining room and covered porch is a nod to the additions of so many houses whose multiple, turn-of-the-twentieth-century porches were slowly incorporated as interior space over time. A jog that connects part of the rear addition to the main house is punctuated with two differently sized diamond-paned windows, an intentional quirk that hints at some long-ago structural evolution. In adding these details, we sought to give this house the history it deserves.

Along the way, in raising, rebuilding, and moving the house, we discovered some of its actual origin story. Our great find was a skeleton of centuries-old timbers. This 1700 house was supported by massive, hand-hewn beams, some of them more than 30 feet (9 m) long. While we no longer needed these to provide the underlying structure, they were the missing link to the home's past, hiding beneath walls and cladding. We carefully removed and sorted the beams, then repurposed them to stretch across bedroom ceilings and to give character to the kitchen and dining rooms. In the end, the newest volumes of this house are supported by its oldest parts.

Throughout, we balanced history with our own trove of new design ideas. We chose windows that are hand

built in Maine, with traditional weights and brass chains. We built guest bedroom closets as millwork cupboards, mirroring the built-ins from eighteenth- and nineteenth-century houses. We used unlacquered brass for all our door hardware, so it would patinate naturally. But we also designed and had built a sleek brass and glass china cabinet that we placed directly over an eight-part window. We favored hanging light fixtures designed by Florian Schulz in the 1970s. We put slabs of marble wainscoting on the kitchen walls. Perhaps our biggest departure from history was a sensuous ribbon of a stairway, with brass spindles and a banister that curved from cellar to attic floor.

The house we created, both in excavating its history and helping it along with an invented one, feels as authentic as any other we've done. If we have succeeded, it will be because our hand is nowhere to be seen; that a passerby fully believes Palmer Cottage was always thus. In designing a traditional house, there is terrific vindication in that anonymity.

Home Tour: Old Within New

JUST AS WE DID WITH THE ARCHITECTURAL DETAILING, WE knew we'd have to use interior design to give this house a sense of history. And while traditional details like moldings and paneling echo those of our other houses, we worked hard to add quirks and imperfections to give the house a sense of depth and age. We did this by upping the dial on texture (sheepskin, lots of low lighting, and plenty of aged and imperfect objects). But mostly, our approach was to give each room its own story. What does this room want to be, and how does it feel unique? Those are the questions we asked as we laid out each space.

Opposite: The entry hall view into the den and first-floor primary bedroom beyond.

THE KITCHEN

One of the advantages of substantially adding on to the house was the ability to rethink the flow of rooms. In East Hampton, we were always challenged by the fact that the kitchen was so removed from the main living areas. Here we made the kitchen the fulcrum of the ground floor, with openings directly onto the living and dining rooms. This configuration left the outside corner of the house as the kitchen's only two walls: one is the front facade, with a perfect secondary entrance to the house, and a shallow, inset porch that borrows from the one in our previous East Hampton house; the other, at the back of the kitchen, needed windows, if only for the exterior façade views. And so, with all four sides of the kitchen given over to room openings or windows, we had no obvious wall for cabinets or storage.

Our solution was a dramatic one: we decided to punctuate that back wall with an eight-part window, evocative of a traditional Tudor window arrangement. Directly in front of that huge expanse, we commissioned a brass and glass cabinet to hold our dishes, glasses, and other objects.

Though in general our project at Palmer Cottage was to add historical detail where there was none, we didn't bring anything into this kitchen that screamed "old-timey." There aren't many great ways to make a kitchen feel old, and precisely because this is the heart of the main floor, we instead opted for the kitchen-that-isn't-a-kitchen. In many ways, this room is our Brooklyn kitchen writ large, inspired by that rear parlor's repurposed bookcase and side bays. A 16-foot (5 m) island holds the sink and stoves, and most of the storage, just like in Park Slope. Similarly, it allows for a large entertaining area that faces, but is separate from, the work areas.

Avoiding the McShingle

Over the last twenty years, houses have sprouted in the Hamptons as potatoes once did. Like the McMansions found all over the country in newly stamped-out luxury developments, these "McShingles" are a supersize take on the traditional Hamptons cottage. If anything kept us up at night, it was the fear that we would accidentally create such a monster. The secret to avoiding such a fate is paying attention to two things: quirk and restraint. Old houses have a feeling of being old because they have evolved over time. Adding elements such as a few uniquely sized windows or asymmetrical wings helps give a house an irregular, imperfect quality. And resist the urge to make everything as big as the law—or your budget—will allow. Instead, aim for proportion. We learned this through trial and error, tweaking the volumes and room sizes and removing elements like a planned additional dormer. Fairly late into our renovation, after seeing the first-floor rooms framed out, we made the opening from the kitchen to the dining and living rooms smaller. This created a greater separation between the three rooms, giving each of them a more intimate sense of scale, and preventing the space from reading as one overly large great room.

Previous pages: By placing the minimalist Gaggenau cooktop and sink in the island and hiding the fridges behind millwork panels, we helped the kitchen kind of disappear.

Opposite: Cleo Baldon stools from the 1960s sit in front of the kitchen island. Brooklyn artist Evan Yee created the massive brass and glass china cabinet.

Above: Like in Brooklyn, we favored open
storage here for our collection of antique
copper cookware. The counter and oak
shelves above the Gaggenau ovens are also
home to electric appliances and vintage
kitchen linens.

Opposite: Twin VOLA faucets in unlacquered
brass are minimal but jewelry-like in their
precision and form, and will develop a lovely
tarnish over time.

THE DINING ROOM

The rear addition is meant to evoke a once-larger porch that had been partially enclosed at some point in history, and its glassed-in portion has the feel of a winter garden. Because our favorite part of our East Hampton dining room was its abundant winter light, this room called out to be just that.

We aren't formal dining room people, so we designed this room as a kind of extension of the kitchen. We anchored each side with two 12-foot (3.7 m) custom black linen English roll-arm sofas. One provides half of the seating for a proper dining table (five vintage Hans Wegner Wishbone chairs line the other side). The other serves as a banquette for a lounge area and is accompanied by a couple of low round coffee tables and French deco tub chairs. Though the dining room isn't used as often as other living areas, giving it another purpose ensures that it has life in it. The result is a space where we start and end each day: coffees in the morning and cocktails at sunset.

Borrowing from Restaurants and Hotels

Some of our favorite spaces to learn from aren't other homes. Our dining room draws inspiration from Ilse Crawford's Swedish hotel Ett Hem, where the dining room is multipurpose, doubling as a library and lounge. In the den, we channeled the subtle use of color in Roman and Williams's SoHo store and café, the Guild and La Mercerie (see page 242 for an interview with cofounder Robin Standefer).

Opposite: A double Posa chandelier by Florian Schulz complements its sister version in the kitchen. We commissioned the 12-foot (3.7 m) oak table in the manner of a 1930s Utö console by Axel Einar Hjorth.

Following pages: A pair of custom English tight-back sofas in black Belgian linen runs the length of full-height dining room windows and faces a collection of French deco tub chairs, re-covered in curly sheepskin. As in all the rooms, the shapes and colors play off one another here: the strong black rectangles of the windowpanes and the long linen sofa are a counterpoint to the roundness of the sheepskin chairs and oak cocktail tables.

THE LIVING ROOM

One of Pilar's bêtes noires is the tyranny of the
TV. Many people have come to expect a television
in every room. We have fought against that trend,
refusing to have one in the main space of any of
our houses. But TV or not, it's awfully nice to
lounge in this room, so having really comfortable
sofas is something we've cottoned to. Here we
placed a long bouclé sofa in the style of Jean Royère
facing the fireplace, then arranged some of our
favorite pieces around it to create gracious and
elegant conversation areas. Guillerme et Chambron
chairs, a Hans Wegner daybed, and a pair of Poul
Kjærholm daybeds around the room unite these
separate arrangements with a common palette of
sheepskin, leather, oak, and neutral colors.

   One of the big decisions we made that departed
from the East Hampton house was to break up
a wall of French doors. The beauty of a bank of
French doors is its ability to allow the whole wall
to open up to the outside. Practically speaking,
we never did that. So here we separated a pair of
doors on each side with a giant multipaned picture
window in between. The fixed window not only
allows for more practical furniture arrangement
inside, it also invites plantings outside. A parterre
with varied sizes of boxwoods feels like it's almost
inside the house and allows this space to act as a
garden room in any season.

Right: A pair of Guillerme et Chambron Grand
Repos armchairs in shearling wear leather
head pillows that nod to the vintage leather
daybed by Poul Kjærholm. The two-piece
travertine coffee table is 1970s Italian.

Above: A collection of brass and leather
objects forms a simple tableau on the coffee
table. The stool is a vintage Poul Kjærholm,
and the walnut tripod lamp in the background
is from BDDW.

Opposite: A pair of French 1930s tub chairs—
upholstered in curly sheepskin—sits behind a
daybed by Hans Wegner.

Following pages: A view into the living room
from the kitchen: a bouclé sculptural sofa is
flanked by French oak cocktail tables. The two
vintage brass helmet lamps are originally from
a 1960s yacht. The Enzo Mari *Apple and Pear*
print and the stair's ebonized handrail provide
a graphic punch.

VIP GUEST ROOM

Increasingly, we see the need for (and popularity of) a bedroom on the first floor. We situated one in a new wing we added to the east side of the house, cladding the exterior in painted wood, rather than the cedar shingles used for the rest of the house. We also added a seamed copper roof. It will take about thirty-five years for the copper to turn a verdigris green color, something we kind of love because it will be a sign of age and patina long after we've moved on from this home.

Inside, we again tackled the windows-versus-millwork problem we faced in the kitchen. Here we had a bank of windows and French doors on two exposures, with the interior wall reserved for the bed. So where to put a dressing room or expansive closets and not block the sunrise exposure to the east? We decided on a central fireplace, flanked by two generous double-hung windows. Then we built a whole wall of book-matched white oak to serve as the chimney breast, window seats, bookcases, and lots of closet storage. In the end, it's probably the most striking room in the house because of the sheer expanse of oak, and the warmth it exudes in any season.

Left: We planned the first-floor guest room so that it could also serve as a primary bedroom—an acknowledgment that someday we might not want to climb the stairs to bed. For the Mario Papperzini iron chairs, we made French mattress-style cushions.

Following pages: We hung a large Isamu Noguchi Akari lamp in the first-floor guest room. Original beams support the vaulted ceiling. The brass fireplace fender is nineteenth-century English.

Above: The custom ribbon staircase—with its ebonized railing, brass spindles, and custom brass turnbuckles—winds its way from the lower level up to the attic floor.

Opposite: Hallways can be dark afterthoughts. In most new floor plans, whether for economy or efficiency, priority is generally given to bedrooms. We had enough of those, so we reserved a generous bank of windows on the south facade to serve as a wide gallery, with a French library table and Cleo Baldon director's chairs.

Opposite: Rosewood and cane Plexus chairs by Illum Wikkelsø anchor the gallery.

Above: A view into the primary bedroom. The wall-mounted valet is by Poul Østergaard.

THE PRIMARY SUITE

In our primary bedroom suite, as with the first-floor bedroom, we raised the ceiling to expose the hip roof gable, and braced it with original beams that we found during the house's restoration. In both rooms, we hung the moon—or, specifically, a very large Noguchi light sculpture. And in both, we commissioned a canopy bed in oak, to add a little romanticism to these heightened spaces. The primary suite also has one feature we borrowed from East Hampton: a shallow balcony overlooking the pool. We've never understood large second-floor terraces—often underutilized and windy spaces. A solution looking for a problem, if you will. But a balcony large enough for us to enjoy coffee in our bathrobes, or to allow us to fling open the French doors for maximum breeze and light, is a glorious perk.

Right: A Børge Mogensen writing desk in white oak offers a delicate perch, with some of the best views of the gardens.

Making Bathrooms Less Bathroomy

After doing many bathrooms all in tile, in this house we decided to opt for baths that feel more like rooms. We continued the oak floor from the rest of the house, adding paneling detail to the walls. Shaded sconces replace the typical glass ones, to make the rooms feel like they might have been converted to baths a century ago instead of newly constructed as wet rooms.

Opposite: When it comes to doorknobs, go small and unlacquered. Smaller doorknobs read more historically accurate, and raw brass quickly develops a patina that is both rich and feels like it has endured the elements for decades.

Above: We paired Lefroy Brooks fixtures in silver nickel with brass lighting and hardware. The walnut stool by Charles and Ray Eames was originally designed for the Time-Life offices in New York.

THE THIRD FLOOR

In many ways, we salvaged this house for its third
floor. Today's building code forbids a habitable
third floor, which makes these dormered rooms so
prized and such a symbol of a historic house. When
we stripped back the walls and ceilings of ours, we
found the first of the original eighteenth-century
beams. They formed a series of upside-down Vs,
each pinned at its point with a large wood peg.

　　This is also where we found remains of the
home's original subfloor—pine planks, some as
wide as 24 inches (61 cm). To honor the original
details on this top floor, we decided to fashion
just two rooms, separated by an open landing
and reading nook. We thought of these rooms as
gracious New England college dormitories.

Above: Mitered shiplap covers the many-
angled walls and ceiling of a third-floor
guest room.

Opposite: In the attic bedrooms, diamond-
paned French casements and oak writing
desks nestle into the south dormer nooks.

OUTSIDE

One of our town's modern building code
requirements—and a good one—is energy efficiency.
Faced with the necessity of adding solar panels
to offset our house's electricity consumption, we
struggled with how to install these important bits
of technology without ruining the historic nature
of our shingled roofline. The solution was to create
a modernist tennis pavilion. This long, rectangular
building, designed to be more Palm Springs than
Hamptons, provides a flat roof sized exactly to
accommodate our twenty-four panels. Inside, we
sheathed the ceiling in mahogany, matched with a
custom cooking island on one end and a fireplace
and lounge area on the other. By using a Turkish
marble for the flooring, as well as for the pool
surround and patio, we made a decisive departure
from the ubiquitous bluestone patios of the area.

Opposite: As an homage to famous Parisian parks, we created a long allée of hornbeam trees set in pea gravel, which shades the 20-foot (6.1 m) table and benches we had made for this epic outdoor dining room.

Above: The modernist tennis pavilion, with its outdoor kitchen and separate dining and lounge areas, is a design departure from the main house, but it borrows the same flared column detail.

Getting the Old-House Details Right

Reading books, taking drives through old neighborhoods, and referencing historic architects are the best ways to ensure that a new house or addition stays true to its origins and era. We studied Joseph Greenleaf Thorpe, the master of the shingle-style houses from the turn of the twentieth century, as inspiration for the detailing of everything from window placement to roof overhangs.

Above: At the pool patio, with its backdrop of 'Limelight' hydrangeas and flanked by magnolia kobus trees, vintage 1950s iron furniture by Mario Papperzini (collected piece by piece from auction houses all over the country) and fringed patio umbrellas complete the nod to the Slim Aarons era.

Opposite: The balcony of the primary bedroom suite caps a covered porch off the dining room.

Bridgehampton

Design Notes

∧ RH SYLVAIN SOFA This white bouclé sofa, a riff on Jean Royère's Polar Bear sofa, is a perfect counterpoint to the angles of the travertine table and daybed in our living room.

< CABLE-KNIT CASHMERE PILLOWS No matter how minimal or traditional a sofa or space, you can always make a case for an arrangement of neutral-colored cashmere pillows and throws.

∧ PALMGRENS LEATHER BOXES We first fell for this traditional Swedish leather goods brand in Stockholm, namely for their leather and caning handbags. They also do these beautifully made leather boxes in different sizes and colors. We, of course, love them in the untanned bridle leather.

> ENZO MARI PRINT We love the graphic nature of this print that hangs over the living room fireplace. It also nods to the *Apple* and *Pear* prints in the kitchen of our house in Brooklyn.

∧ FARROW & BALL PAINT Throughout the house, we selected a single family of Farrow & Ball grays to accent the white trim and black window casings but maintain some relation to one another. We used Worsted (left) in the laundry room and Ammonite (right) in the dining room.

∧∨ SHEEPSKIN UPHOLSTERY One of our signatures is the use of curly sheepskin as upholstery fabric. With each home, we have gotten more daring, and more willing to splurge, in how much we use it. Not all pieces can stand up to shearling upholstery—its thickness tends to hide subtlety of shape, so we use it when we're going for soft, curvy shapes rather than harder edges. We get ours from Dualoy in New York.

∧ WHITE OAK FLOORS For the floors, we opted for 8-inch (20 cm) planks of quartersawn white oak with a Nordic finish that gives the floorboards a pale hue. (We even used white oak in bathrooms; it is warmer underfoot than tile, and gives the rooms a more living room–like, less utilitarian feel.)

> ANTIQUE KAZAK RUG We joke that this rug is our *Where's Waldo?* moment. This well-worn antique lived in the entrance of Pilar's childhood home and has made an appearance in just about every house we've ever owned. Don't underestimate the value of putting old things in a house that's largely new.

< ∨ FRONT DOOR RIM LOCKS These
elevate a front door. Their simple shape is
modern, and they're obviously a great piece
of historical design.

< ∧ SMALL KNOBS We used unlacquered
solid brass hardware from Baldwin
throughout the house, and we always size
down—smaller knobs are historically
accurate and have a great hand feel. (We used
a 2-inch/5 cm knob for passage doors and
a 1¾-inch/4.5 cm knob for closets.) Though
lever-style handles on the French doors
might be more practical (the knobs' center
placement on the French doors makes them a
bit of a knuckle breaker), we love the subtlety
of a knob over a lever.

< ∧ CLASSIC BRASS PULLS The quality of the hardware
from Classic Brass—a small Jamestown, New York, company
founded in 1946—is unrivaled. We used the Aspen series
in brass (also shown above, in chrome), which feels both
nautically chunky and jewelry-like.

> LITTLE HARBOR WINDOWS When it comes to restoration, windows are everything. While in previous homes we were lucky enough to be able to salvage a few original wavy-glass diamond-paned casement windows, there were only two windows in this house worth saving, which we ended up using in our uninsulated outbuildings, where energy efficiency was less of an issue. A fellow Hamptons designer turned us on to a small family-run custom window maker based in Maine. They made all 120 custom mahogany windows for the house. The double-hung windows have the exposed traditional weights and chains mechanism, and the French casements (right) have traditional brass pushers and stays. We painted them with a thin coat of black, so the fine grain shows through, but opted to keep the insides of the frames unpainted, which is both a nod to the historical method of keeping the "travel area" unpainted for better glide and to show off a bit of the raw mahogany.

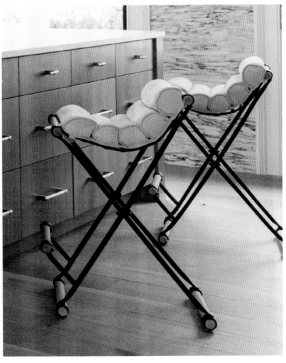

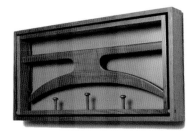

∧ POUL ØSTERGAARD WALL VALET More ornamental than practical, this teak wall valet from the 1960s makes a cameo appearance in all our homes. We think of it as functional art.

< CLEO BALDON IRONWORK BARSTOOLS We reupholstered this California designer's 1960s stools and director's chairs in Sunbrella chenille.

∧ POUL KJÆRHOLM DAYBEDS We have long coveted the Kjærholm daybed in bridle leather, which has skyrocketed in value over the past twenty years. We were thrilled when we found a pair of them that had some serious patina (more than most people are comfortable with, frankly, but which we love).

< DANSK SALAD BOWL Teak is the preferred wood for Danish furniture, and its oily nature makes it perfect for serving bowls, which prevents them from drying out after repeated washings.

∧ POUL KJÆRHOLM STOOL This is a rare collectible, especially in bridle leather. It's essentially a piece of sculpture that pinch-hits as additional seating.

∨ MOGENSEN WALL-MOUNTED NIGHTSTANDS We use these any time we need something space-saving. They hit a decidedly modern note with sculptural lines and the absence of legs, which allows them to float.

< ROUND BELGIAN OAK TABLE AND CHAIRS This was a rare, never to be found again, anonymous-designed table and chairs set that we bought at auction in Germany. The table is so beautifully chunky, and the chairs are as elemental, almost primitive, as they are sculptural.

< ∧ FRENCH MATTRESS CUSHIONS
We upholstered the window seats in the
downstairs bedroom, as well as the garden
chairs we ended up putting inside, using the
French mattress upholstery technique. We
opted for Sunbrella fabric for practicality, but
with thick piping and tufting for drama.

< MARIO PAPPERZINI CHAIRS Our
favorite garden chairs, collected piece
by piece from auction houses, are these
Salterini-made ones from the 1960s,
designed by Mario Papperzini. They're
comfortable but spare, and a nice departure
from the ubiquitous teak furniture often
seen in the Hamptons. Newly made versions
can be found from the British company
Heveningham.

∧ NICKEY KEHOE OAK COFFEE TABLES You
can't go wrong with these solid oak low, round
coffee tables. They're a modern interpretation of a
Pierre Chapo table. You can dress them up with brass
objects or stacks of books, or leave them spare for
hyperutility.

> DIETER WÄCKERLIN CREDENZA The exterior
of this minimalist credenza gets its warmth from
the walnut. Inside, it's a jewel box of cabinetry
details—pale birch pullout drawers with Tiffany
blue accents and even a pullout drinks caddy.

Borrowing from the Best

LIKE SO MANY INTERIOR DESIGN JUNKIES, WE HAVE SPENT countless Sundays over the years poring over stacks of shelter magazines and monographs for inspiration. (We still keep a physical folder filled with dog-eared tear sheets, some dating to the 1990s, as well as virtual folders saved in our Instagram archives.) And while we admire a wider range of styles than is reflected in our decorating choices, we find that we return again and again to a handful of designers for their deft layering of periods, palettes, and textures. Nate Berkus, Joseph Dirand, Sean MacPherson, Thomas O'Brien, Tom Scheerer, Robin Standefer (of Roman and Williams), and Pierre Yovanovitch, while each totally distinct, all share a mastery of a certain push-pull between the traditional and the modern, the warm and the sexy, old and new. From Nate Berkus, Thomas O'Brien, and Tom Scheerer, we learn that it's only by being a rigorous student of design that you can successfully break the rules, whereas as from Sean MacPherson and Robin Standefer, we understand the value of the theatrical and of hitting various "notes" in a single space. Joseph Dirand and Pierre Yovanovitch teach us that sometimes you have to reinvent the narrative of a home in order to find its most authentic design expression. These designers, whose quiet (and sometimes not so quiet) irreverence evolves our eye by challenging conventional design wisdom, give us permission to take creative risks of our own.

In the following pages, these friends and mentors generously open up their playbooks, offering tips, inspiration, and hard-earned wisdom.

Nate Berkus

Nate Berkus Associates, Chicago

LEAD WITH YOUR LIFE STORY.

For me, the only successful interiors are
the ones that tell the story of the people
who live there, whether subtly or overtly.
Over the last twenty-five years, I have felt
that my primary responsibility as a designer
is to figure out how to tap into a dialogue that
allows a personal narrative—who my clients
are as people, what their family histories are,
how they parent, where they've traveled—to
bleed into a space.

EVERY CHOICE SHOULD BE PERSONAL.

As my eye moves around a room, I'm always
struck by the memory of a person, place,
or time—with whom, where, or when I
acquired something. Over the years, I've
found that it's the pieces that are meaningful
to you, that you have a real connection to,
that give a room its life.

Above: The double-height living area in Nate
Berkus and Jeremiah Brent's West Village
home

Opposite: The range hood, backsplash, and
countertops in Berkus and Brent's West Village
kitchen are made out of Calacatta marble.

REPURPOSE TEXTILES AND FABRICS.

Those textiles that you couldn't resist buying in Marrakech but that have been stashed in a closet for a decade can become upholstery for a chair. An old cashmere cable-knit sweater with a moth-eaten sleeve can become a throw pillow. It's about not only using what's vintage but also giving a second life to something that's beloved. These little moments of patina add such character to a space, especially in new architecture.

MAKE SURE THERE'S JUST ENOUGH IMPERFECTION.

You have to bring in things that are made by hand, things that are imperfect. It's important to see the soul of certain objects, to see the craftsmanship in the weave, the dye lot, the braid, or the maker's hand in a piece of pottery.

TOO MUCH GOOD CAN BE BAD.

It's not enough to fill your home with expensive things. A museum-like space with the best-in-class example of a certain era of art or furniture design falls flat and is ultimately just really uninteresting. One of the ways that I've worked in tandem with clients who have a strong connection to a certain period or furniture maker is to mix in craft—you'll see across a lot of my work a ton of basketry or handwoven fabric. Or I'll create tension by upholstering a really fine French chair from 1950 not in shearling or camel wool but in an old textile from a Turkish or Mexican flea market.

Joseph Dirand

Joseph Dirand, Paris

PAY ATTENTION
TO NATURAL LIGHT.

When we bought our apartment, I responded to the light as it evolved throughout the day. We have the sunrise in our living area, so we kept the space white and bright. Whereas for the bedroom behind the kitchen, which doesn't get direct sun, I went with more beige and warmer tones to match the intimacy of the space.

KEEP THE PALETTE
SIMPLE.

I use a lot of stone and marble, as well as molding and paneling, and very little paint. While the palette is really simple and muted, there is a lot of texture.

PAY ATTENTION TO HOW YOU ACTUALLY LIVE.

You can't have aesthetics alone driving things. The role of good design is to create a reassuring, comfortable envelope for your life. We used to have a beautiful dark Jeanneret dining table, but it removed all the light from the room. When we changed it to a white table, the candlelight played off it and transformed the whole mood. These things—the sense of life around the dinner table—you discover little by little as you study how you go about your day.

DON'T BE AFRAID TO CHANGE THE STRUCTURE.

In my own apartment, I added these massive stone arches, the kind you would find in a much bigger home, to create a link between the spaces. I also added a lot of molding and cabinetry, which looks like it's always been there. I like to create dialogue and surprise between rooms.

MINIMALISM DOESN'T MEAN EMPTY.

While I'm a minimalist, I'm attracted to strong materials, strong brutalist forms, and strong architecture. I also love the romanticism that comes with curves. It's when you combine these things with a neutral palette that spaces become really interesting.

KITCHENS CAN LOOK LIKE ROOMS.

We used monolithic materials in a poetic way, like instead of a straight hard-edged counter, it's round. It's a functional room, but it's also like a living room because it's where we spend most of our time with family and friends.

Opposite, left: The bedroom in Dirand's current Paris apartment

Opposite, right: A view into the eat-in kitchen of the designer's previous home

Above: The use of stone is a Dirand signature, as seen in the massive marble coffee table in his living room.

Sean MacPherson

Co-owner of independent hotels, New York

SHOW THE HUMAN HAND.

Navajos deliberately sew a mistake into everything they make, as a kind of acknowledgment of the imperfection of life. Given the homogenization of design, I believe that seeing human fingerprints and human foibles is more powerful than ever—in terms of the actual objects, and the point of view of the design. Imperfection is key.

MAKE IT HIGHLY PERSONAL.

I would much prefer to be in a place that I don't necessarily love from a design perspective but that feels personal to the individual who owns it than be in a space done by a big-name decorator who has little connection to the owner. I am lucky enough to have grown up in California in the 1970s with a surfer mom. Some of my projects, like the Park, speak to that hippie rebellious culture that was so rich in craft. We are all so touched by our childhood experiences and formative years that we either replicate or reject what we grew up with.

DO YOUR RESEARCH.

The problem these days is that "good taste" has been democratized by the internet and social media. In an age when everyone has access to a lot of the same references and buying sources, the only way to create original spaces is to keep evolving your eye and your references and inspirations. The definition of sophistication is having more knowledge and, in terms of design, being confident enough to try new things.

Opposite: The lobby drawing room in MacPherson's Marlton Hotel in Greenwich Village

Above, left: It's all rosewood and navy blue at the nautical inspired Maritime Hotel.

Above, right: Another view of the wood-clad lobby at the Marlton

Thomas O'Brien

Aero Studios, New York

GOOD DESIGN STARTS
WITH GOOD COLLECTING.

All the things you look at, touch, use, live with—from flatware to books to a little stack of linen napkins—is the real landscape of a home. Sometimes I am searching for something to fill a corner of a room, but more often than not it's the other way around: I find a certain piece of brass hardware or an oak table with a certain leg detail and it becomes the inspiration for a space. And while I have a lot of valuable pieces, I find as much pleasure in a humble brass hardware fixture from the nineteenth century that I've picked up for a dollar. I am always looking for a certain goodness or utility, corny as that might sound, that you find in anything made of solid materials.

saying every room should be a combination of both—even in the most seemingly traditional spaces, like the "Library Bedroom," where hanging over a pair of ornately carved nineteenth-century American mahogany pineapple-post beds is a set of Cy Twombly lithographs from 1980.

TAKE INSPIRATION FROM YOUR HOME'S HISTORY.

When I bought the Academy, I uncovered the space's history—in this case, three generations, the original of which dated back to 1833, when it served as a boys' school. I started collecting pieces from all different stages of the building's construction, like nineteenth-century antiques and industrial elements from the 1920s and 1930s (which was around the time when the second owner, a poet named Anne Lloyd, moved in and built the additions that give the home its current footprint).

BE A FOREVER STUDENT.

I know a lot about the dishes, flatware, and all the other things I find and collect, because I study them. I spend a great deal of time with various experts in different design periods—

. . . BUT DON'T BE BOUND TO IT.

When I restored the Academy, I more or less maintained the volume of the original classroom. I custom designed a clean steel-framed table but surrounded it with a mix of traditional and modern seating. I'm always

Opposite: The living room/work space in Thomas O'Brien's 1833 restored schoolhouse in Bellport, Long Island, called the Academy

Above, left: A Hamptons house designed by O'Brien mixes modernist architecture with vintage pieces.

Above, right: A view into the kitchen of O'Brien's Library House, which the designer built from scratch adjacent to the Academy

Above: The living room of O'Brien's long-held
Manhattan apartment

Opposite: The office of O'Brien's husband, designer
Dan Fink, in the Library House

dealers, millworkers, restorers. I'm so impressed with every knowledgeable person whom I've learned something from, like this guy who cornered the market on Seth Thomas clocks and knew everything about them. It's an ongoing education that I try to share with my clients.

LET A HOUSE GROW WITH YOU.

My approach with clients is to try to get people to imagine that the house will be in a family for 150 years, to understand that it's a process, rather than thinking about it in terms of "just make it be done on this day." Hopefully they are engaged enough along the way so they can walk people through the home and talk about their choices and the history behind the house and the furnishings with a sense of ownership of the process, not just the end product.

INVEST IN INTERIOR ARCHITECTURE, NOT JUST INTERIOR DESIGN.

There is a big difference between decorating and informed decorating, which requires more skill and an understanding not just of fabrics, furniture, and paint color but of real interior architecture, of how rooms are used and relate to one another. I want to teach people how to spend their money well, on smart things like custom windows, great millwork, moldings, hardware—those seemingly invisible things that you can't always put your finger on but that make a difference.

PRIORITIZE COMFORT.

So much of my work is in figuring out how something can be lovely but also feel good and easy; how it can be special and normal at the same time. This takes a lot of time and consideration. I think through the everyday, like how you reach for a utensil drawer in a kitchen, or how people cook and spend time together, or hang out in the kitchen even if they don't cook. When I was doing restaurants in the beginning with Brian McNally, he would often say, "You know, you can't make it too tricky." Like you can't put the bar just anywhere. It just doesn't work. There are some rules that we follow because it has to make sense.

Tom Scheerer

Tom Scheerer Incorporated, New York

EXPENSIVE DOESN'T NECESSARILY MEAN SPECIAL.

No matter how upscale the project, I always go to little mom-and-pop antiques stores like Sage Street in Sag Harbor and buy a four-dollar dish or something and throw it in. People often think everything has to be expensive, and it's just so not true. Without incorporating a few things that are inexpensive but that you love, you are going to get that overly sanitized luxury look that is in some ways, ironically, the very opposite of sophisticated.

TOO MUCH OF ANYTHING IS, WELL, TOO MUCH.

There's nothing more deadly than rooms that are too strict, too period. A room full of art deco furniture (no matter how much I love deco furniture) is stultifying if there's too much of it.

START WITH WHAT'S ALREADY THERE.

Whether for my personal projects or my clients, I always like to take my cues from something that's already in the space and transform it. Even a funny paint color can become a starting point, which you might improve upon with a slightly different hue.

A GOOD NARRATIVE NARROWS THE UNIVERSE.

I don't just say, "Oh, this is going to be the aqua bedroom." There has to be a reason, which is why I work with clients to craft a story ahead of time. Sometimes a painting, like one I found with a little bit of blue in it that felt like it belonged in a certain bedroom, becomes the inspiration for the room's paint color. Having a story imposes a certain discipline. It allows you to eliminate a lot of stuff that you might have been attracted to because it didn't follow the story—a kind of antidote to the tyranny of choice.

EMBRACE DISSONANCE.

Part of the job of the decorator is finding that common thread between disparate objects—between a Chippendale side table and a Thonet chair. I can't write poetry, but it's a similar exercise in terms of finding these kinds of dissonances and similarities.

PERFECT IS NO FUN.

I grew up in traditional homes, so when I'm doing these grand houses in places like Maine, East Hampton, or Southampton, I like to bring a little bit of my family history to it and introduce to them some quirks that I learned from my ancestors, little things that give a house its necessary idiosyncrasies.

Opposite: The living room of Scheerer's historic Paris apartment, located on the Île Saint-Louis

Above: Scheerer's bedroom salon wall in his uptown Manhattan apartment

Robin Standefer

Roman and Williams Building and Interiors, New York

BE AGNOSTIC.

Roman and Williams Guild [the furniture design studio Standefer cofounded with her husband, Stephen Alesch] is centered around surfacing a global community of artisans and craftspeople working at the highest level. It is about bringing everybody together with a common philosophy around furniture and housewares that are not just beautiful but also highly usable. The idea is to bring down barriers between people from different places, different walks of life, and different nationalities through craft and design. There can be so much creativity in how you mix and match different traditions and vintages even at the dinner table—not only in a culinary sense but also with our dishware: French glassware with Japanese bowls. There is something quintessentially American about being open to so many different cultures.

LIVE WITH YOUR HEIRLOOMS.

It was Martha Stewart who many years ago said when she saw my collection of Dylan Bowen and Martin Pearce that ceramics, too, could be heirlooms. I'd never used the word to describe those pieces before she said it because I thought of an "heirloom" in terms of an antique grandfather clock or something. But heirlooms, I have come to realize, can be anything that holds value to you that you pass on.

BUY WHAT YOU ACTUALLY LOVE.

I collect things because I love them, and some are worth a lot and some I picked up for less than a dollar. I'm so tired of people wanting the Pierre Jeanneret chair, which is a wonderful simple chair that's become totally outrageously expensive because it's been made popular by celebrities. I always encourage people to buy something with more character that's braver, more interesting; that's challenging.

MATERIALS MATTER.

Oak, brass, and saddle are so much a part of the modern (and ancient) story of craftsmanship. Brass and oak in particular have been used for centuries for applications

like flooring, plumbing, and hardware due to their durability and the simple fact that they don't rust—during the preindustrial era, people had to have things that had that kind of strength, longevity, and character. And then, of course, they became part of some unbelievable traditions in the twentieth-century, post–industrial revolution, when they took on fanciful and extraordinary forms. Stephen and I talk a lot about making pieces in materials that pull a thread through history, even as they get reimagined for modern use. Because while there is a spontaneous kind of beauty around these materials, there is also a history and nobility.

Opposite: The Roman and Williams–designed Veronika restaurant at New York's Fotografiska Museum

Above: La Mercerie, the restaurant within the Roman and Williams Guild furnishings store

LIBERATE YOURSELF FROM DESIGN LINGO.

I have been challenging myself at the mood board stage to sit and write down real words, adjectives, or metaphors beyond design that tap into the senses and get at qualities I want a house to have. Like when we did the Boom Boom Room and André [Balazs] said when he saw our initial concept, "I just love the idea that you feel like you're inside of a jar of honey." And I said, "Yes, maybe it's a jar of honey with a Bentley detail." This is especially helpful for people who aren't in the design world, rather than labeling themselves as "modern" or "traditional," because the truth is most of us are looking for a bit of both. And yet, most of what's out there forces us to choose, which is where people get stuck. So if instead you think about how you want a room or a corner to feel— cool, warm, smooth, whatever—and start associating colors and fabrics that bring that feeling to life, then you have a starting point. I always tell people to create a mood board of five things they really love, which can be anything from their grandma's teapot to a modern chair. This way, you'll put together pieces that talk to one another, not because of their design era but because of their feeling, material, or craftsmanship.

LET YOUR DESIGN SHOW ITS AGE.

People have this perception that modern has to be new, but at the core of our practice is a modernism that's allowed to age. And so our perspective on modern has always had to do with this idea of "living finishes"—it's so important for us to work with natural materials that breathe, grow, and change. We might do a soap finish on oak where you still see the grain, but we don't suffocate it with a catalyzed lacquer.

Above and left: Standefer and Alesch's Montauk house

Opposite, top: The Boom Boom Room atop the Standard Hotel, dubbed by many as the sexiest bar in New York City

Opposite, bottom: The upholstered banquettes at La Mercerie

GIVE A SPACE A BREATHER.

Even if you like rich, layered spaces and heavy, honest pieces, as Stephen and I do, there is a value in feeling and seeing the silence between things. We might love the density of muscular oak tables, but we also love the counterpoint of open space that allows what's there to get the spotlight.

or even industrial. The magic in the design is that you can hit these notes even within a single space, with the material as the common thread that allows the different elements to speak to one another.

STRIVE FOR VARIETY
WITH UNITY.

Oak can be a lot of different things. When it's pickled or oyster shelled, it goes pale and modern. It can be waxed and get kind of ruddy, like a hardworking French farm table. It can have lots of different personalities, yet it's still oak, which is brave, strong, and warm. Brass when polished can go flashy and sexy, but when it's oxidized, it can go rustic

Pierre Yovanovitch

Pierre Yovanovitch, Paris

YOU CAN BE ELEGANT *AND* PLAYFUL.

There is something paradoxical about true elegance. It must be simultaneously understated and outstanding, a mix between wisely predictable and wildly original. It is also lighthearted. One could say that my work in Fabrègues [his house in the south if France] is nothing but an attempt at elegance. My approach is to a large extent subconscious. I try to start each project with my intuition and imagination. There is a story to tell, in some cases that of my clients, in others that of fictional characters (such as one of my favorites: Mrs. Oops) or that of the house or its environment. I try to avoid systematism in order to stay free.

during the summer. Instinctively, I set out to re-create a place that would live all year round. For example, the fireplace had been replaced in the nineteenth century with one that was rather too small for the size of the room and a little boring. So I worked with one of the last *gypsiers* (*gypserie* is the traditional craft that made elaborate moldings in Provence) to re-create what the original fireplace could have been (erring on the side of exuberance, because it was the story that I wanted to tell). In the process, we did extensive research on seventeenth-century Provençal *gypserie* and made sure that our design paid respect to the architecture and the history of the building. So we did work within the beauty and constraint of the existing architecture and at the same time took some liberty in interpreting it.

RE-CREATE WHAT SHOULD HAVE BEEN.

My house was originally built in 1620 on a site where the family had already lived for centuries. In the twentieth century, it became a summer vacation place for the family's descendants and was somewhat neglected. It had lost its vibrancy and was some kind of a sleeping beauty only visited for two months

Opposite: In the living room in Pierre Yovanovitch's home, Château de Fabrègues in Provence, Arnold Madsen's Clam armchair, circa 1945, sits in the foreground.

Above, left: The spare primary bedroom with original twelfth-century beams

Above, right: Yovanovitch rebuilt the fireplace with a local artisan.

Above: A chair by James Mont in the library of
Yovanovitch's sprawling estate

Opposite: A sprawling built-in sofa, in oak and mohair

MIX DESIGNERS AND TRADITIONS.

I have a deeply rooted love for the era of Swedish Grace, a not-so-well-known design movement of the 1920s. Gunnar Asplund, whom I consider to be one of the greatest Swedish architects of the first half of the twentieth century, was part of this decorative movement, as was Axel Einar Hjorth. Rigor, balance, curves, depth of materiality were characteristics of the furniture pieces from this era. They were often very simplistic with an organic, raw quality (pinewood), but there were extremely sophisticated elements to them, too (wood marquetry). They are remarkable.

I also look up to Nordic designers from the 1930s and 1960s such as Frits Henningsen, Paavo Tynell, and Flemming Lassen, and American designers like Paul László, Paul Frankl, Terrence Harold Robsjohn-Gibbings, James Mont, and Harvey Probber.

Mid-century American designers knew how to overturn convention: steel, cork, ceramic, wood with numerous editions in variations of these materials not necessarily found in Europe. Paul Frankl's cork and oak coffee table is fascinating. I like the strength and authenticity of design from this mid-century American era. The architecture of this time showcased originality without ostentation or arrogance with an exactitude that is timeless.

RESPECT CRAFTSMANSHIP AND MATERIALS.

When it comes to material choice, at the heart of everything is my commitment to craft and longevity. As a part of this, I work to utilize natural fibers (wool, linen, silk) and local,

responsibly sourced woods (produced locally to promote short supply chains, from eco-certified forests; FSC, PEFC) in our furniture. In this way, there is a natural look to the materials that blend in together and set the stage for the bolder elements of the space.

WORK UP TO BOLD COLOR.

My approach to color has evolved over time. I started with a relatively neutral palette so the colorful artwork and furniture in the space could really shine through. Over the years, I have moved to a bolder palette and gradually added stronger hues in the rooms, most noticeably the main living areas. I've learned that a carefully selected bold color can often be a better setting for art than a neutral one and that the use of strong colors is very satisfying.

The Masters

A SURVEY OF

TWENTIETH-CENTURY DESIGNERS

THROUGHOUT OUR PROJECTS, AND OVER ALL THESE YEARS, our tastes have evolved. And so what began with a fascination with the usual suspects—Danish modernists like Arne Jacobsen and Hans Wegner— led us down a rabbit hole of ever more obscure designers like Brazilian Jean Gillon, whose groovy organic forms wouldn't have caught our younger eye. Our appreciation for a diverse mix of styles and moods, for quirks and whimsy, for the variation of texture and craftsmanship—even for things that on some level challenge our notions of "good taste"—all of that has been the fun part of the ride. What follows is an unapologetically subjective survey of one hundred modern designers from the 1930s to the 1970s.

Danish

JOHANNES ANDERSEN

1903–1991

HB20 credenza

GÖSTA BERG

1903–1993

Seagull chair

RAINER DAUMILLER

(dates unknown)

Bench

NANNA DITZEL

1923–2005

Egg chair

PREBEN FABRICIUS

1931–1984

and JØRGEN KASTHOLM

1931–2007

Scimitar chair

OLE GJERLØV-KNUDSEN

1930–2009

OGK chair

PIET HEIN

1905–1996

Barstools

FRITS HENNINGSEN

1889–1965

Sofa

POUL HUNDEVAD

1917–2011

Guldhøj folding stool

PETER HVIDT

1916–1986

and ORLA MØLGAARD-
NIELSEN

1907–1993

Secretary

ARNE JACOBSEN

1902–1971

Seagull chair

BÖRJE JOHANSON

(dates unknown)

Barstools

FINN JUHL

1912–1989

Pelican chair

EDVARD KINDT-LARSEN

1901–1982

and TOVE KINDT-LARSEN

1906–1994

Tove sideboard

ERNST KÜHN

1890–1948

Bar table

JACOB KJÆR

1896–1957

Chair

SVEND LANGKILDE

(dates unknown)

Bar cabinet

POUL KJÆRHOLM

1929–1980

PK24 chaise

FLEMMING LASSEN

1902–1984

Chair

AKSEL KJERSGAARD

(dates unknown)

Dresser

MOGENS LASSEN

1901–1987

ML42 stool

KAARE KLINT

1888–1954

Red chair

ARNOLD MADSEN

1907–1989

Clam chair

MOGENS KOCH

1888–1992

Bookcase

BØRGE MOGENSEN

1914–1972

Spanish chair

KAI KRISTIANSEN

b. 1929

Troja chair

NIELS MØLLER

1920–1981

Model 62 chair

KURT ØSTERVIG

1912–1986

Bar cabinet

BERNT PETERSEN

1937–2017

Stool

ARNE VODDER

1926–2009

Credenza

OLE WANSCHER

1903–1985

Egyptian stool

HANS WEGNER

1914–2007

GE 375 Paddle chair and ottoman

ILLUM WIKKELSØ

1919–1999

Plexus chair

KAI WINDING

(dates unknown)

Dresser

French

JACQUES ADNET

1901–1984

Chair

ADRIEN AUDOUX
and FRIDA MINET
(dates unknown)

Chair

PIERRE CHAPO

1927–1987

Bookcase

MICHEL DUCAROY

1925–2009

Togo sofa

CHARLES DUDOUYT

1903–1969

Credenza

RENÉ GABRIEL

1890–1950

Chair

ROBERT GUILLERME

1913–1990

and JACQUES CHAMBRON

1914–2001

Grand Repos chair

RAYMOND LUNEL

d. 1978

Wall light

RENÉ MATHIEU

(dates unknown)

Wall light

PIERRE PAULIN

1927–2009

Big Tulip chair

CHARLOTTE PERRIAND

1903–1999

Double wall light

JEAN PROUVÉ

1901–1984

Lacquered bench

JEAN ROYÈRE

1902–1981

Polar Bear sofa

JEAN TOURET

1916–2004

Table

Italian

FRANCO ALBINI

1905–1977

LB7 bookcase

MARIO BELLINI

b. 1935

Le Mura lounge chair

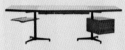

OSVALDO BORSANI

1911–1985

Desk

ACHILLE CASTIGLIONI

1918–2002

Snoopy table lamp

SILVIO CAVATORTA

(dates unknown)

Credenza

GIANFRANCO FRATTINI

1926–2004

Chair

IGNAZIO GARDELLA

1905–1999

T2 dining table

ANGELO LELII

1911–1979

Triennale floor lamp

FABIO LENCI

b. 1935

Hyaline chair

ANGELO MANGIAROTTI

1921–2012

Eros table

LUIGI MASSONI

1930–2013

Jumbo Line bookcase

ROBERTO MENGHI

1920–2006

Table lamp

GIUSEPPE OSTUNI

(dates unknown)

243 table lamp

ROBERTO PAMIO

b. 1937

and RENATO TOSO

b. 1940

Lara sofa

WILLY RIZZO

1928–2013

Bar

CARLO SCARPA

1906–1978

Kentucky chair

TOBIA SCARPA

b. 1935

Soriana sofa

ALDO TURA

1909–1963

Bar

MARCO ZANUSO

1916–2001

Senior chair

Swedish

CARL-AXEL ACKING

1910–2001

Vanity

PIERRE FORSSELL

1925–2004

Candleholder

JOSEF FRANK

1885–1967

1063 Tutankhamun stool

AXEL EINAR HJORTH

1888–1959

Utö table

HANS-AGNE JAKOBSSON

1919–2009

B-138 table lamp

UNO KRISTIANSSON

b. 1925

and ÖSTEN KRISTIANSSON

1927–2003

Wall mirror

CARL MALMSTEN

1888–1972

Samsas chair

GUNNAR NYLUND

1904–1997

Bowl

Swiss

WILLY GUHL

1915–2004

Loop chair

PIERRE JEANNERET

1896–1967

Chandigarh chair

UBALD KLUG

1932–2018

Terrazza sofa

DIETER WÄCKERLIN

1930–2013

B41 credenza

Austrian

CARL AUBÖCK

1900–1957

Carafe

Belgian

JOSEPH FRANÇOIS DE COENE

1875–1950

Display cabinet

German

FLORIAN SCHULZ

(dates unknown)

Table lamp

Dutch

GERARD VAN DEN BERG

b. 1947

Rock sofa

Finnish

PAAVO TYNELL

1890–1973

9459 wall lights

American

WARD BENNETT

1917–2003

I-Beam table

JOHN DICKINSON

1920–1982

Africa table

PAUL EVANS

1931–1987

Cityscape desk

VLADIMIR KAGAN

(born in Germany)

1927–2016

Serpentine sofa

WALTER LAMB

(dates unknown)

Sled chair

GEORGE NAKASHIMA

1905–1990

Minguren 1 table

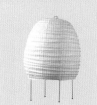

ISAMU NOGUCHI

1904–1988

Akari table lamp

WILLIAM PAHLMANN

1900–1987

Sideboard

MARIO PAPPERZINI

(dates unknown)

Chairs with ottomans

TOMMI PARZINGER

(born in Germany)
1903–1981

Cabinet

HARVEY PROBBER

1922–2003

Architectural Series chair

EERO SAARINEN

(born in Finland)
1910–1961

Tulip table

Brazilian

JEAN GILLON

(born in Romania)
1919–2007

Bertioga chair

OSCAR NIEMEYER

1907–2012

Rio chaise

SERGIO RODRIGUES

1927–2014

Tonico chair

JORGE ZALSZUPIN

(born in Poland)
1922–2020

Presidencial chair

Thank you.

TO HENRY AND WILLEM, FOR YOUR PATIENCE WITH MOVING (and moving the furniture) at your parents' whim, and for putting up with the constant patter about doorways and tile and such.

To Lia Ronnen, for your support and faith from the very beginning. And our eagle-eyed, multi-hyphenate, indefatigable editor, Bridget Monroe Itkin—you made this book infinitely better on all fronts. And to the rest of the talented team at Artisan.

To our families. Gregg and Andrea, for being our partners in renovating and cohabitating—a social experiment if ever there were one, and a family love we couldn't imagine living without. Beverly and Allan, for your faith in, if occasional exasperation with, your aspirational son. Anna, for your unwavering love for your daughter, even when her financial leaps shook you to your core. And Claudio, our muse and inspiration. If only you were still with us, you'd be the most enthusiastic player in these crazy adventures.

To our collaborators. Monica Nelson, for your elegant eye. You realized our vision and added your own. Adrian Gaut, for your inimitable sense of light and detail. Andrea Chu, you are quite literally our resident artist and documentarian. François Dischinger, Martien Mulder, and Matt Hranek, for capturing form and life in architecture and design. Emilia Vincent, Tony Freund, and the world-class dealers at 1stDibs, for the inspiration, education, and imagery.

To the makers. Tamer Pepemehmetoglu, you're our partner who allows us to dream bigger. Anne Sherry, for your architectural temperance and quiet grace. Roel Miguel, we are in awe of your gifts as a builder and an artisan. Evan Yee and Manuel Sinchi, for coaxing such beauty out of raw material. Gilmer Ramirez, Amilcar Miguel, Hector Miguel, Isaias Mendaz, Paul Kayel, Bob Teodoru, Johnny Cardona, and Andrew Camp, we are deeply grateful for your camaraderie, your talent, and your commitment to excellence. Geoffrey Nimmer and Aaron Marchese, for teaching us that the design outside is as important as what's inside. And Frank Newbold and Beate Moore, for your wise counsel and constant cheering.

And, finally, a nod to these historic structures themselves. Whether enjoyed by our family or others we have passed the keys to, they will reflect the passage of time, in ways both accumulative and degradative. The patina of love, loss, and above all, memories.

—PILAR & CHRIS

FURNITURE CREDITS

All images here provided courtesy of 1stDibs, a site for vintage, antique, and contemporary design. See below for 1stDibs dealer information.

PAGE 88: Kaare Klint Addition sofa: Wyeth; Hans Wegner Daybed for Getama: Danish Modern L.A.

PAGE 89: Travertine Table by Up&Up: Studio Cadmium

PAGE 92: Carl Auböck objects: Original in Berlin (candle sconce) and Modernisten (carafe)

PAGES 98–99: Utö table: H. Gallery; Lassen chair: Flavor; Series 7 chair: Almond & Co; Daumiller bench: Eneby Home; Juhl bench: Adam Edelsberg; Chapo bookcase: Goldwood Interiors; Luxus mirror: Nordlings; Wegner desk: Ponce Berga; Hunting chair: Modern50; Pelican chair: Dada

PAGES 102–103: Onos lamp: Original in Berlin; display cabinet: Modernisten; nautilus shell lamps: Mass Modern Design; Red chair: Milsted Andersen; three-drawer desk: Joseph Berry Interiors; Parzinger tall cabinet: Modern Epic Antiques; fireplace fender: elmgarden; Lunel articulating brass wall lamp: Fins de Siècles; Petersen rosewood stool: 50/60/70; Addition sofa: FK Gallery

PAGES 106–107: PK24 wicker chaise: De Angelis; Daumiller dining set: FCK Paris New York; Nakashima coffee table: Adam Edelsberg; Tulip table: Patina NYC; Egyptian stool: Carl Hansen & Søn; Auböck tray: HPS Design Interior; Terrazza sofa: Goldwood Interiors; oak stools: Contemporary Showroom; oak chair: Automaton

PAGES 110–111: Hein barstools: Automaton; Scarpa sofa: AFD Warehouse; Groovy chair: Modern-ID; Libra-Lux lamps: Nekonato Gallery; Bambole sofa: Mass Modern Design; Hillebrand mushroom lamp: Lomomomo; Serpentine sofa: Stamford Modern; Lenci chair: Milord Antiques; PK80 daybed: Secher Fine Art & Design; Eros table: Pavilion Antiques

PAGES 114–115: Dudouyt credenza: Piet Jonker Architectural Antiques; Dickinson table: Dragonette Limited; Stalagmite table: Milord Antiques; Snoopy lamp: Flos; Tura pedestal bar: Modern Design Connection; Tonico chair: Forsyth; Jangada chair: Melides Art; Evans patchwork metal coffee table: 20cdesign; Gatta wall lamp: Bloomberry

PAGE 159: Arnold Madsen Clam chair: Dagmar

PAGE 226: Poul Kjærholm daybed: Secher Fine Art & Design; Mogensen wall-mounted nightstands: Justine

PAGE 254: HB20 credenza: Machine Age, Boston; Berg Seagull chair: JF Chen; Daumiller bench: Eneby Home; Egg chair: Another Classic ApS; Scimitar chair: Frank Landau Selected Design Objects, Fine Art & Interior Design; OGK chair: Skovshoved Møbelfabrik; Hein barstools: Automaton; Henningsen sofa: Studio Schalling; Hvidt and Mølgaard-Nielsen secretary: Holm Vintage; Jacobsen Seagull chair: Orange Furniture; Johanson barstools: Studio Schalling; Pelican chair: Dada

PAGE 255: Tove sideboard: Gallery Wernberg; Kjær chair: Ponce Berga; PK24 chaise: De Angelis; Kjersgaard dresser: Galerie Bachmann; Red chair: Milsted Andersen; Koch bookcase: Milsted Andersen; Kühn bar table and Langkilde bar cabinet: Studio Schalling; Lassen chair: Flavor; Clam and Model 62 chairs: Dagmar; Spanish chair: Milsted Andersen; Østervig bar cabinet: Walter Design

PAGE 256: Petersen stool: 50/60/70; Egyptian stool: Carl Hansen & Søn; GE 375 Paddle chair and ottoman: Forsyth; Winding dresser: FK Gallery; Audoux and Minet chair: soyun k.; Chapo bookcase: Goldwood Interiors; Togo sofa: The Loods; Dudouyt credenza: Piet Jonker Architectural Antiques; Gabriel chair: Timothy Brown Studio; Grand Repos chair: Pavilion Antiques

PAGE 257: Lunel wall light: Fins de Siècles; Mathieu wall light: Original in Berlin; Big Tulip chair: Artbrokerdesign; double wall light: Two Enlighten Los Angeles; Prouvé lacquered bench: Archeologie; Touret table: Robert Stilin; LB7 bookcase: Pescetta Home Decoration; Le Mura lounge chair: Archive 20th Century; Borsani desk and Cavatorta credenza: Mass Modern Design; Snoopy lamp: Flos; Frattini chair: Morentz; T2 dining table: Forsyth

PAGE 258: Triennale floor lamp: soyun k.; Hyaline chair: Milord Antiques; Eros table: Pavilion Antiques; Jumbo bookcase: Tante Eef Design; Menghi table lamp: Stamford Modern; 243 table lamp: Two Enlighten Los Angeles; Lara sofa: Walter Design; Rizzo bar: Morentz; Kentucky chair: Pescetta Home Decoration; Soriana sofa: AFD Warehouse; Tura bar: inside-room; Senior chair: 50/60/70

PAGE 259: Acking vanity and Kristiansson wall mirror: Nordlings; Forssell candleholder: Doctor Decorum; 1063 Tutankhamun stool: The Exchange Int; Utö table: H. Gallery; Loop chair: Siècles de Brocante; Chandigarh chair: Galerie 54—Eric Touchaleaume; Terrazza sofa: Goldwood Interiors

PAGE 260: Auböck carafe: Modernisten; De Coene display cabinet: Morentz; Schulz table lamp: HPS Design Interior; Rock sofa: Mass Modern Design; 9459 wall lights: Two Enlighten Los Angeles; I-Beam table: Neal Beckstedt Studio; Dickinson Africa table: Dragonette Limited; Cityscape desk: Converso; Serpentine sofa: Stamford Modern; Sled chair: The Modern Vault

PAGE 261: Minguren 1 table: Adam Edelsberg Akari table lamp: Two Enlighten Los Angeles; Papperzini chairs with ottomans: Tom Robinson Modern; Parzinger cabinet: Modern Epic Antiques; Architectural Series chair: Matthew Rachman Gallery; Tulip table: Patina NYC; Bertioga chair: Studio Designboard; Rio chaise: Equinoctial; Tonico chair: Forsyth; Presidencial chair: Peter Blake Gallery

PHOTOGRAPHY CREDITS

COURTESY OF AERO STUDIOS: Page 90 (book cloth lamp)

COURTESY OF BALDWIN HARDWARE: Page 224 (front door rim lock and small knob)

COURTESY OF BDDW: Page 158 (tripod lamp)

COURTESY OF NATE BERKUS: Pages 230–231

ANDREA CHU: Pages 34, 36, 44, 46, 47, 50, 51, 64–65, 70, 71, 77, 86 (tableau and Japanese textile), 87, 88 (leather banquette, top), 89 (Arne Jacobsen Swan chair, Kay Bojesen Danish teak monkey, and Goop x CB2 love seat), 90 (folk art rabbit, Hans Wegner Cow Horn chair, and Osvaldo Borsani desk for Tecno), 91 (Guillerme et Chambron dining chair), 92 (bisque porcelain vases, Raymond Loewy Script, and Pierre Forssell for Skultuna objects), 93, 112, 160 (Kaare Klint Safari chair), 160 (Belgian footed bowl, right), 161 (Thomas O'Brien Long Box sconce and bar cart, left), 191, 204–205, 218–219, 222 (RH Sylvain sofa), 224 (Classic Brass pulls, left), 225 (Cleo Baldon ironwork barstool), 226 (Dansk salad bowl), and 227 (French mattress cushion)

COURTESY OF CLASSIC BRASS: Page 224 (Aspen pull)

JOSEPH DE LEO: Pages 157 (Lindsey Adelman Knotty Bubbles chandelier) and 158 (Lindsey Adelman Branching Bubble chandelier)

ADRIEN DIRAND: Pages 232–233

FRANÇOIS DISCHINGER: Pages 8–9, 117, 122–123, 125, 126–127, 128–129, 130, 131, 133, 134–135, 136–137, 138–139, 140–141, 144–145, 148–149, 150–151, 158 (Series 7 Arne Jacobsen chairs), and 159 (butterfly stool and Black Forest mounts)

YOLANDA EDWARDS: Page 216

COURTESY OF FARROW & BALL: Pages 86 (Elephant's Breath) and 223 (Worsted and Ammonite)

COURTESY OF 1STDIBS: Pages 88 (Kaare Klint Addition sofa and Hans Wegner daybed for Getama), 89 (travertine table by Up&Up), 92 (Carl Auböck objects), 98–99, 102–103, 106–107 (all but the Akari lamp), 110–111, 114–115 (all but the brutalist vase), 226 (Mogensen wall–mounted nightstands), 254–261

JÉRÔME GALLAND: Pages 246–249

ADRIAN GAUT: Pages 4, 5, 18–19, 22, 23, 26, 27, 28, 30, 31, 32, 35, 38, 43, 45, 49, 52–53, 54, 55, 57, 58–59, 60, 61, 62, 63, 67, 68–69, 72, 73, 74, 75, 76, 79, 80–81, 82, 83, 84, 90 (Borsani P40 chair), 91 (naval scissor lamp, bottom), 96, 100, 104, 108, 115 (brutalist vase), 164, 168, 173 (bottom), 177, 187, 188–189, 195, 196–197, 198–199, 200, 201, 202–203, 206–207, 208, 209, 210, 211, 212–213, 214, 215, 217, 218 (left), 221, 223 (white oak floors and sheepskin upholstery, bottom), 225 (Little Harbor windows), 226 (Poul Kjærholm stool and round Belgian oak table and chairs), 227 (French mattress cushions, left, and Dieter Wäckerlin credenza), 232, 250, 251, 264, and 265

MATT HRANEK: Pages 88 (Enzo Mari prints), 89 (Kay Bojesen Danish teak animals, right), 91 (George Nelson Bubble lamp), and 174

THE ISAMU NOGUCHI FOUNDATION AND GARDEN MUSEUM, NEW YORK / ARS: Page 107 (Akari lamp)

FRANCESCO LAGNESE: Pages 237 (right), 239, and 241

COURTESY OF SEAN MACPHERSON: Pages 234–237

CHRIS MITCHELL AND PILAR GUZMÁN: Pages 40–41, 118, 119, 120, 121, 146–147, 155, 156 (rush-handled basket, left), 157 (Illum Wikkelsø Plexus oak and cane chairs and John Derian Field Bench), 159 Arnold Madsen Clam chair, right), 160 (Belgian footed bowls, left), 161 (bread boards and bar cart, right), 173 (top and middle), 181, 182, 220, and 223 (antique Kazak rug)

MARTIEN MULDER: Pages 12–13, 175, 180, 183, 192, and 193

MONICA NELSON: Page 224 (front door)

COURTESY OF NICKEY KEHOE: Page 227 (oak coffee table)

COURTESY OF PALMGRENS: Page 222 (leather box)

COURTESY OF POTTERY BARN: Page 156 (rush-handled basket, right)

JAKE RAJS: Pages 142–143, 152–153, and 154

COURTESY OF RALPH LAUREN HOME: Pages 156 (cable-knit blanket) and 159 (Westbury sconce)

LAURA RESEN: Pages 236, 237 (left), and 238

COURTESY OF ROMAN AND WILLIAMS BUILDINGS AND INTERIORS / ROMAN AND WILLIAMS GUILD: Pages 242–245

RICHARD TAVERNA: Pages 179 and 184–185

SIMON UPTON: Page 240

COURTESY OF DAVID WEEKS: Pages 88–89 (chandelier)

INDEX

Library of Congress Cataloging-in-Publication Data

Names: Mitchell, Chris, 1970– author. | Guzmán, Pilar, author.
Title: Patina modern : a guide to designing warm, timeless   interiors / Chris Mitchell and Pilar Guzmán.
Description: New York : Artisan, 2022. | Includes index.
    Identifiers: LCCN 2022010979 | ISBN 9781648290558
    (hardcover)
Subjects: LCSH: Interior decoration—Psychological
    aspects.
Classification: LCC NK2113 .M58 2022 | DDC 747—dc23/
    eng/20220413
LC record available at https://lccn.loc.gov/2022010979

Design by Monica Nelson

Artisan books are available at special discounts when purchased in bulk for premiums and sales promotions as well as for fund-raising or educational use. Special editions or book excerpts also can be created to specification. For details, contact the Special Sales Director at the address below, or send an e-mail to specialmarkets@workman.com.

For speaking engagements, contact speakersbureau@workman.com.

Published by Artisan
A division of Workman Publishing Co., Inc.
225 Varick Street
New York, NY 10014-4381
artisanbooks.com

Artisan is a registered trademark of Workman Publishing Co., Inc.

Printed in China on responsibly sourced paper

First printing, October 2022

10 9 8 7 6 5 4 3 2 1